THE CONSPIRACY OF
GOD
THE HOLY SPIRIT IN MEN

THE CONSPIRACY OF
GOD

THE HOLY SPIRIT IN MEN

JOHN C. HAUGHEY

DOUBLEDAY & COMPANY, INC.

GARDEN CITY, NEW YORK

1973

ISBN: 0-385-00400-1
Library of Congress Catalog Card Number 73-80730
Copyright © 1973 America Press, Inc.
Printed in the United States of America
First Edition

TO MY DAD

Contents

Preface by Leon-Joseph Cardinal Suenens   ix

I   *Jesus of Nazareth and the Spirit of God*   1

II   *From Following Jesus to Being Led by the Spirit of Jesus*   40

III   *The Personality of the Holy Spirit*   69

IV   *Contemporary Spiritualities and the Spirit*   96

V   *Who Is Duped, Who Spirit-Led?*   118

Preface

Books on the Holy Spirit are rather rare in the Catholic Church of the Latin rite. The Fathers of the Eastern rites who were present at Vatican Council II never ceased to remind the rest of us that our preparatory schemas had failed to accord a sufficient amount of attention to the Holy Spirit. These were, in their judgment, theologically deficient texts since they lacked a pneumatic dimension. An effort was made during the Council, in working out the definitive texts, and after the Council, when the texts for the Eucharistic liturgy were being revised, to give more attention to the place of the Holy Spirit in Christian life. We remain deficient in this matter even to this day. The Holy Spirit is and remains the very soul of the Church. A Christianity that forgets or construes as old fashioned His active and activating presence will be a truncated Christianity.

Father Haughey offers us a precious contribution, to overcome the inadequate consciousness of which we all are guilty, in his words on the Holy Spirit. He helps us to situate the Holy Spirit in the pre-eminent position from which it will renew the Church and make her young again. His chapters on The Personality of the Spirit, contemporary spirituality and discernment should be enlightening to the reader. Of all his chapters, I particularly appreciate the one in which he establishes the profound and constant connection between Jesus of Nazareth and the Holy Spirit.

With justification, the author points out that in the past we have given in to the tendency to present the mystery of Jesus in terms of a Divine Theophany—God coming *to* us under human appearance rather than *from among* us in the mystery of the Incarnation. We must meet the authentic Jesus, a man among men, conditioned by the relativity of time and space as men always are. Notwithstanding his humanity, he was and is the unique Son of the Father who was led and invested with the power and strength of God by the Spirit. We must see the mystery of the Incarnation and the life of Jesus in the light of the central affirmation of the Credo: "He was born of the Virgin Mary by the Power of the Holy Spirit." To forget or minimize the role of the Holy Spirit is to deform the true countenance of the Lord and compromise his mission.

Having underscored the presence of the Holy Spirit in the Christ, the author invites us to pass beyond an extrinsic notion of imitation of Christ to a more profound one. Hence his chapter on the Holy Spirit as animator of the life of a person, the inner source of the similarity to Christ which is possible for each of us Christians in the Spirit. I detect here the author's faithfulness to the spiritual tradition that goes back to St. Ignatius Loyola and the masters of interiority who were part of that same rich heritage such as Fathers Lallemand and de Caussade.

Father Haughey gives us a modern version of this spirituality, however, by insisting that the interaction between the Holy Spirit and men is one of "conspiration." (The Greeks would have spoken of a divine-human synergy.) He rightly sees that the action of the Spirit does not eliminate men's freedom or in-put or role. God's action penetrates a man in such a way that the élan of a man's choices, actions and living is traceable to the gentle action of the Holy Spirit without, at the same time, ceasing to be also a man's own. His freedom preserved, a man transcends what he could do and be on his own while his person is lovingly respected by God and never diverted from self-actualization. We must learn again and again this way of the Spirit, and it is only the Spirit who can teach us this.

Father Haughey and I have on occasion talked about the Holy Spirit, not as a theological curiosity, but in the evident manifestations of the Spirit's activity in the Church today. We have experienced much convergence of viewpoint and mutual appreciation, in particular about the Charismatic movement in the United States and throughout the world. Although Father Haughey does not speak ex professo about the Charismatic movement which is an astonishing manifestation of the conspiration of the Spirit and men in our contemporary world, his book will be a real service to those who are puzzled about this movement as well as a significant contribution for those who are participants in it. I think that many others who are rediscovering the Holy Spirit will also be helped by it. I see the Spirit animating the broad phenomenon of communally shared prayer and behind the many attempts at renewal of the Church through communities radically orienting themselves to the Gospel.

We are, I believe, on the threshold of a spiritual spring-time in the Church. These pages will help Christians who are desirous of becoming young again through the Holy Spirit to do so in continuity with the tradition of the Church. They might even be an occasion for wel-coming with joy the Spirit who alone can renew at the depths of our needs, the face of the Church and the world.

Malines   June 1973

✠ L.-J. Cardinal SUENENS,
Archbishop of Malines-Brussels

THE CONSPIRACY OF
GOD

THE HOLY SPIRIT IN MEN

Jesus of Nazareth and the Spirit of God

There seems to be a growing curiosity in the Christian community about the Holy Spirit. Some are just puzzled, many are interested in knowing more, and a growing number are enthusiastic since they claim to have discovered new dimensions to their faith through a new experience of the Spirit. As with any of the claims others make or questions we ourselves have about God and His ways with us, we are always well advised to begin our inquiry at the nearest point of access we have to the Godhead: Jesus Christ. Our relationship to the Spirit will depend on and be illumined by Jesus' relationship to the Spirit.

But if the way we have tended to see Jesus in the past has not led us to understand or give much attention to the Spirit, then there must be some deficiency in how we have looked on Jesus. For this reason, our inquiry in this chapter will be at the same time critical of our past understanding of Jesus and an attempt to understand his relationship with the Spirit.

Classical Christology managed to articulate an understanding of Jesus that dwelt on ideas about his two natures without giving sufficient attention to the role of the Holy Spirit in his developing self-understanding. A Jesus who is imaged as having made it without the Spirit generates a piety in which the Spirit is superfluous for all practical purposes. Hence, the need to spell out the role of the Spirit in the life of Jesus of Nazareth.

Periodically we are treated with explanations for Christianity's perennial condition of anemia. Secularization, with all its nuances, seems to be the favorite contemporary explanation. Whatever the explanation, the solution for overcoming the anemic condition is usually considered the same: Have a stronger faith. I would like to submit another explanation and offer a different solution. The pedestalization of Jesus is the main reason for the anemic condition of Christianity. The process of pedestalization began as early as the time that the New Testament itself was being formed and it has persisted throughout the centuries. Pedestalizers assume that the more unlike us Jesus is made out to be, the more awesomely we will look upon him. They seem to think that belief in him flourishes the less his similarity to us is emphasized. When the relationship between Jesus and the Spirit is clarified, pedestalization of Jesus will be seen as a false way of honoring him, a dishonoring, in fact. There are two ways of pedestalizing him: disgorge him from the human condition or ignore his relationship with the Spirit. Jesus can be depedestalized and praised, on the other hand, when he is understood as a Spirit-led man.

Hence, if Christ's pedestalization explains our faith's anemia, a new acknowledgment of the Spirit's operation in Christ and an acceptance of the same role in us could be the beginning of the solution.

We cannot blame Jesus himself for this process that sets him apart from us and eventually aside. He had no pretensions about not being one of us, or feelings that he was unlike us. What he learned about himself, he discovered only gradually. And what he taught he had first to learn.

Someone who did not go from ignorance to knowledge, from doubt to certainty, from indecisiveness to decision, through trial and error, analysis and insight, was undoubtedly remarkable, but was not like the rest of us. He should not be offended if we have a difficult time identifying with him and no interest in following him. The great misfortune of the Christology bequeathed to us is its portrayal of a figure who effortlessly knew; from the beginning of his Incarnation he had nothing to learn, just much to teach.

Jesus is not praised by those who call him Lord unless they first know and never forget that he is also their brother, the first of many brothers, maybe, but brother nonetheless, and this he will be for all eternity. The only homage that does him justice is that in which he is raised up from within the human order which he, in turn, raises up and glorifies. If the price we are paying for glorifying him is disparagement of ourselves, if belief in him requires disbelieving ourselves, his death has cost something he never intended.

3

a. Under the Tutelage of the Spirit

Jesus learned the way every human being learns except that his principal teacher was the Spirit. Some of the means used by the Spirit were the same ones available to every other Jew. The difference was that, whereas Israel was under the mediation of the Law, Jesus was under the immediate tutelage of the Spirit. Nevertheless, the Spirit taught him by means of the Law, the prophets, and the prayers of the Chosen People. From his earliest years he regularly heard the Word of God in the synagogue of Nazareth as well as repeated continually by the devout. From his mother, he learned how to ponder in his heart these treasured records of God's ways with men. One of the most frequent signs of Christians' pedestalization of Jesus is a disparagement of the faith of the people of Israel. By so doing they ignore the fact that he was product of and heir to what the Spirit had been doing in Israel for the long centuries of its development. The New Testament shows unmistakably Jesus' reliance on Israel's prayer, her sacred traditions, and her faith. The Spirit guided Jesus, not in spite of these elements of Israel's sacred traditions, but by means of them.

God would have been untrue to Himself and spiteful of the work of His hands if Jesus had come from outside and to Israel rather than from within the bowels of Yahweh's Chosen People. It was with the realization of her being the Chosen of Yahweh that Jesus came to see that he was the Chosen One, the new Moses, who was to lead

4

his people out of bondage, the Prophet who was to teach
the people how infinitely more loving than the dreams of
their old men and the visions of their young their God
was. The fact that he transcended Israel in his chosenness
and yet came from within her revealed the constancy of
the Father's plan and a faithfulness that was from everlasting to everlasting. If Jesus did not come from a people, he was not a person and our following of him is a
charade. If he did not spring from the bowels of Israel
then God was deceived in choosing Israel or ineffectual
after He made His choice. But this is not the case, of
course. The power of the Most High that overshadowed
her enabled Mary to choose from within and on behalf
of Israel that for which Israel had been chosen.

Perhaps there was something even more important
than any of the means already cited, that the Spirit used
to teach Jesus his identity. Through the relationships
that developed between Jesus and others, the Spirit
taught him. A capacity for being in relationship with another or others in such wise that one comes to self-
understanding through these is by no means automatic
or universal. Relationship in this sense means a quality
of betweenness that exists when two people are present
to one another as who they are. There are degrees of
presence to one another or degrees of mutuality in relationships. There can also be false relationships, ones in
which I am present to the other according to the other's
expectations of me or according to my expectations of
the other. There are exploitative liaisons, too, which
simulate the experience of relationship but serve merely
to widen the moat around the person and others and

5

deepen the division between the authentic self and the performing self.

Every genuine relationship is a gift of God and opens out to God. Each deepens one's ability to receive the presence of the other as other. At the same time it develops one's ability to be fully present to another as oneself. Thus, each true relationship expands one's capacity to stand in openness to God as wholly other.

It should prove fruitful, I think, to try to understand the relationship between Jesus and his Father in terms of presence. But even before the full presence of the Father as Father could be experienced by the son, there had to be a capacity in Jesus for relationship, or an ability to be wholly present to the other as oneself and fully receptive to the otherness of the other. In this connection, his mother presumably played an enormously important role. In fact, the significance of her virginity may pale in importance by comparison to her ability to accept the complete otherness of her son without erasing any of his uniqueness which she could not fully understand. Scripture takes note of Mary's capacity for pondering events and others' words. She makes room in her heart for the words of men and angels that speak of unexpected things. She receives them in their otherness. Having made room in her heart and mind for that which was other, she accepted that which was incomprehensible to her, and the Word of God became incarnate in her womb. She understood presence then, in a way she had never before experienced.

But the act of conceiving and giving birth to Jesus was merely prologue to and had to be complemented by her

6

subsequent relationship to him. Her whole being made room for him first in her womb and then interpersonally. He, in turn, developed his own immense capacity for receiving and being present to the other, first of all from his mother. In time, of course, he perceived that the Other into whose Presence he was more and more intimately being led, was his Father. Jesus became consciously son as he grew more capable of being present to his Father as who He was. Mary is the instrument the Spirit used to bring about the union of God with man and Jesus with his Father.

The role of the Spirit is peculiarly directed to the area of intersubjectivity, creating a betweenness where there was isolation. In each of the instances we are dealing with here, it is the Spirit who made the presence of one to the other possible. The words of the Lucan angel Gabriel can apply both to what the Spirit effects in Mary *vis-à-vis* Jesus and to what is effected in Jesus *vis-à-vis* his Father: "The Holy Spirit will come upon you and the Power of the Most High will cover you with Its shadow" (Lk. 1:35).

④ → A Spirit-knit relationship makes the uniqueness of each person ever more distinctive. Jesus' knowledge of God and his knowledge of himself grew apace. The more certain he became that God was loving, the more he knew he was loved. As the personality of God became manifestly that of a loving Father, Jesus learned that he was a beloved son. With infinite skill, the Spirit taught him to differentiate between himself and others, and understand that he was a son in a way no one else ever was or would be. He discovered who he was by discovering that God was his Father. Some of the most important years, therefore, for Christians to reflect on in the life of Christ are the hidden years before his public life. These were not simply endured by him, as a "hanging around" until he would acceptably age to the point that he could proclaim the Kingdom. Rather, they were the years in which the Spirit taught Jesus who he was, that he was child, son, only son of his Father. To one who is like us in all things save sin, such disclosures would have been staggering had they not come gently and in stages.

In a sense, therefore, the Father becomes Father when there is a complete acceptance of His presence by his son. And Jesus becomes the only son of the Father when he freely accepts the full presence of the Father to him as Father. There had to be a *fiat* from him as a man in order for his Father's eternal choice of him as His son to become a reality.

In time the son came to want what his Father wanted. But his Father wanted "all perfection to be found in him," and so it was. This came about not in spite of Jesus' human will but through it. Why should Jesus have enjoyed less freedom than his own mother whose "Be it done to me according to your Word" made his own nativity possible? Because of the full presence of the Father to the son the "fullness" from which we have all received came to rest in the son. END

To sum up, then, Jesus begins to illumine the distinctiveness of the new economy by the way he himself comes into relationship with God and men. The role that the Law had played in the Old Covenant the indwelling Spirit was to play in the new economy of salvation. The

8

end point was the same, that is, union with God. But the
means to achieve this end are unequal. Unfaithfulness
in the old economy manifested itself either by non-
observance of the Law or by a self-righteousness that
sought to manage God's sovereignty by an external observance that inured the person against union with God.
Unfaithfulness in the new economy of salvation shows
up another way. By a failure to observe the greatest of
the commandments, the only law there is: "Love one
another!" one shows his non-cooperation with the activity
of the Holy Spirit. Spirit-knit relationships assume a central place, therefore, in the new economy, since each of
these develops a capacity in the person to receive the
presence of the other in his otherness and vice versa.
Union with God presumes, and in turn, increases our
capacity for relationship with men. By the same token,
Spirit-knit relationships with men sustain and deepen
our union with God. One gets the first glimpses of the
distinctiveness of the new economy in the life of Mary.
But it is in Jesus most of all that we see the workings and
the beauty of the Spirit-gift.

b. The Developing Self-understanding of Jesus

One of the questions that presence-to-the-other poses
and isolates is the meaning of time. Unlike God Himself,
in whom and for whom there are no befores and afters,
we live in a medium of seconds and hours and days. We
are so immersed in it that we tend to be ignorant of time
as a medium. I would suggest that the Gospel expres-

9

sion: "You know not the day nor the hour" could mean that though we may always be able to say what time it is, we do not know what time is. Given the experience of his Father's presence to him and his presence to the Father, Jesus began to perceive how great a gift of his mercy the medium of time is to men and matter. His understanding that his Father's love of him was outside of the medium of time is encapsuled in the statement that enraged his hearers: "Before Abraham ever was, I am" (Jn. 8:58). Jesus came to know in time that the Father had chosen him from all eternity. But this can be a misleading use of words, since it chooses to express in terms of time an experience of the Father's love that supersedes the conditions of time. Quality lamely reverts to quantity for description. By realizing the quality of his Father's love for him, Jesus knew that he was first in every way in his Father's eyes. Before time ever was, this was so.

It is unfruitful to get hung up in the time medium to express the relationship between the Father and His only son. The dichotomy between time and eternity and complex disquisitions on the pre-existence of Jesus rob us of and divert our eyes from the quality of a love that transcends time. Love removes the person from ephemeral enmeshment in hours and years. There is an eternity to it. "All else shall pass away but my love shall not pass away." We have eternal life once we are in relationship to and have accepted the presence of One Who is Indestructible Love. The creature, time, serves its purpose insofar as a deeper and deeper degree of presence has been attained to, since the Love that one then begins to taste has neither end nor beginning. What has always been requires time to perceive, and a number of choices to obtain. Once it has been perceived and fully chosen the scaffolding of time can fall away since Kingdom life has already begun. To the extent the Kingdom is present and realized, there is something unreal and illusory about time.

But to say that Jesus perceived the presence of his Father to him in a fuller and fuller way and chose freely to receive him as his Father is also to say that Jesus was being led and taught by the Spirit. The Spirit's lessons have to do with the developing self-awareness or self-definition of a person. To be in possession of an accurate self-definition undistorted by sin is to enjoy self-knowledge. This knowledge of the self is attained principally through relationships. The "all things" which Jesus himself learned and, in turn, the promised Spirit would teach were realizations in the area of personal identity through intersubjectivity.

The Spirit did not teach Jesus higher math or physics or existentialism. He taught him who he was. Luke describes the development in the young Jesus as an increase "in wisdom, in stature, and in favor with God and men" (Lk. 2:52). He came to see things from the side of God, the way the Spirit and his Father viewed them. Having understood himself and his own heart, he developed an ability which became evident in his public life, of piercing to the hearts of his hearers. He became adept at detecting the dross that had accrued to the work of the Spirit in Israel. He possessed an awesome power of discernment of the religious condition of Israel. But he did not come to a point where he ceased to learn. The author of the Epistle to the Hebrews shows he appreciated this by his remark that Jesus "learned obedience through suffering." He did not arrive at a point when the presence of the Father ceased to be a matter of choice. No, this relationship was something he was continually choosing and just as continuously free to neglect or reject. If he had come to a point during his life where human existence posed no predicament for him, held no mystery for him, or ceased to be a matter of choosing, then he, at that moment, would have ceased to be one of us. Our Savior would have become a poseur at such a moment, one who put up with merely seeming human for our edification.

Judging from the frequency of its mention in the Gospels, the Spirit was at pains to teach Jesus about the Kingdom and his place in it. Not that the Kingdom itself was a place. It was a mode of being, a quality of existence, a condition of life that is the consequence of the intersubjectivity the Spirit authored first and foremost between Son and Father. Jesus did not learn about it in his mind first and then speak about it to men. Before he knew or preached about the Kingdom, he lived the life of the Kingdom by being wholly present as Son to his Father. The Kingdom was a mode of intimacy with God, primarily. Living in the Kingdom meant constantly choosing one's having been chosen. Living in the Kingdom meant loving, because loving and living were synonymous with God. Living in the Kingdom meant that one lived the same life as He lived whose Kingdom it was. Jesus' life was so wholly other as a result of being in the presence of the Father that it was comparable to having been born again.

Kingdom-life, for Jesus, respected all the laws of development that natural life exhibited, not the least of which was growth. So the Kingdom of God was like a seed in the beginning and progressed from there to seedling, to plant, to tree, to glorious fulfillment. The Kingdom began in time but transcended it. It had an existence in time that was a mere hint of the fullness that was to come. There was an eternal quality to it, something that no man could pull asunder of that which the Spirit of God had joined together in time.

Jesus began to see that he was to have a completely unique role to play in the Kingdom. He could see that because of his relationship to his Father, others would be drawn into the Kingdom and take their places in his Father's presence through him. He knew, too, that they could not do this without the same gift from his Father that he received, the Gift of the Spirit. He came to see that all Kingdom things were Spirit things as well as Father things. But most incredible of all, he would come to see that all Kingdom things would in some way come into being through him. He was the door to the sheepfold and Shepherd of the Sheep. To him belonged the keys to the portals, and he was to regulate in some way who would and who would not enter into the awesome presence of his Father.

The Spirit gradually made him privy to the secrets of the Kingdom. It would be, for all practical purposes, Jesus' Kingdom in time. If he had not been taught gently and well, he might have run from so great a responsibility or become presumptuous with the goodness of such a Father.

c. How Jesus Teaches About the Spirit

If the Spirit was all that important and played so cru-
cial a part in Jesus developing a consciousness of his own
identity, how explain the relative silence of Jesus, judging from the Gospels, about the Spirit? Before too readily
conceding an infrequency of mention of the Spirit by
Jesus, one must attempt to understand *how* the Spirit is
mentioned in the Gospels. To rummage through them,
seeking the verses that explicitly mention the Spirit would
be a superficial way of proceeding. Our literalism insults
the Author of the Scriptures, ignores the milieu in which
the New Testament was composed, and misconstrues the
nature of the Spirit's operations.

First of all, the Spirit acts not to point to himself, but to
the Other. In the case of Jesus, the Other was the Father.
With us, the Other the Spirit points to is Jesus and
through him to the Father. Jesus was concerned that his
hearers learn what he was learning, namely, how good
the Father is. His preaching focused on what he had been
taught by the Spirit rather than on the Spirit Himself.
There is a similarity here with any communication between people. We are more concerned to tell others what
it is we have come to understand than how we have come
to understand or by whom we know it. We speak about
the things our faculty of understanding has compre-
hended rather than focus on the faculty itself.

As will be developed later, the work of the Spirit is not
to point to Itself but to witness. So any statement that

Jesus makes about his Father or any work he does in His name is a sign of the presence and power of the Spirit at work in Jesus. The Spirit makes Jesus conscious of the Father, His love and providence, His unreserved largesse toward His son. The Spirit inspires in Jesus a desire for union with his Father in his prayer, in his works, in his will. The Spirit does not develop a Spirit-consciousness as such in Jesus, but an unbroken awareness of union with the Father and a realization that He was constantly saying to him "All that I have is yours." And, of course, the most beautiful thing the Father had to give Jesus (the sign that He would give him all that He had) was the Spirit.

Second, it is the work of the Spirit to fashion the Kingdom. The Spirit had already come to Jesus, but It had not yet come in power to his followers. "The Spirit had not yet come because Jesus had not yet been glorified" (Jn. 7:39). Jesus' way of speaking about the Spirit, therefore, was in part to teach his hearers about that which the Spirit was going to do in them and for them and with them, namely, build a kingdom. All Gospel statements about the Kingdom are teachings about the Spirit. Not the Spirit substantially or in Itself, but functionally and in the effects It will have when Pentecost comes and others will become like Jesus in all things, including being in-spirited.

In Jesus, the work of the Spirit was perfectly embodied. He was the first citizen of a Kingdom that is not of this world. In him one sees the perfect portrait that the Divine Artist is capable of fashioning. God wanted a man to be resplendent with His glory before the Kingdom came in power so that we could have a norm for what the work of the Spirit can be in men and a sign of the splendor that yielding to Its promptings will produce.

But there are several other reasons for Jesus' reluctance to spell out much about the Spirit as such. His hearers would not have considered the Spirit of Yahweh as a distinct personal Being. It was bad enough, this implicit blasphemy that was contained in the hints he was giving about his own identity. He would have been skewered doubly if he had begun to suggest that the Spirit of Yahweh was something more than their Sacred writings had taught them. Their pneumatology had advanced only to the point that saw Yahweh's Spirit as Yahweh's, neither distinct from Him nor personal. It was Yahweh's own dynamism exercised to accomplish His ends. Jesus himself, in fact, would have had the same notions about the Spirit at the beginning of his life as his contemporaries entertained. He would, therefore, good teacher that he was in his own right, have been sensitive to where his hearers were in their understanding of the Spirit. He knew his own Teacher well enough to know that the Spirit would have Its own schedule and Its own way of revealing Its personality to those who would come to believe in Jesus.

But there is a further, more complex reason for the infrequency of mention. The rabbis had taught the people that the Spirit had ceased out of Israel after the death of her last three prophets: Haggai, Zechariah, and Malachi.

It was generally expected, therefore, that there would be no evidence or reappearance of the Spirit of Yahweh until the final times when It would appear tangibly to rest on the person of the Messiah, touching his words and his deeds in such a way that all would recognize his Messianic stature. The Spirit would endow their Messiah with gifts of wisdom and understanding such as Solomon had, fortitude and counsel such as David exhibited, the knowledge and fear of the Lord such as Moses possessed. So Israel believed.

But the expectations about the Messiah became perverted in the course of time. In the hearts of many, the Kingdom that he was to establish was very much a product of their own vanities and cupidity, a creature of time and matter. We must connect, therefore, the reluctance Jesus showed about having himself referred to as the Messiah with the reserve he showed about speaking of the Spirit. In brief, the same reasons he had for preserving the Messianic secret also apply to the pneumatic secret.

One can begin to see the unenviable task in public relations that confronted Jesus. He had to proclaim a Kingdom that did not conform to the expectations of many, maybe most, of his hearers. While trying to straighten out their perverted notions about the Kingdom, he also became aware that, though he was the Spirit-imbued Messiah the people had awaited, the manner of the fulfillment of his task would be as servant. Yet the role of servant of Yahweh was such an unnoticed, unattended portion of the Hebrew scriptures that the people never thought to combine the two figures, Messiah and Servant, into one person, even though each was described in their scriptures as Spirit-filled. A less circumspect proclamation of either the Spirit or his own Messianic identity would have obscured even further what men would have to know to come to eternal life. Having changed as well as he could their notions and expectations about the Kingdom by his words, he came to understand that what he would do in his person would more eloquently proclaim the secret than what he said. By his own free acceptance of the role of Servant of Yahweh and his death, he baptized the notions of Messiah, Spirit, and Kingdom. His death laid to rest not only our sins but our misconceptions also. His gift of the Spirit to us after his Resurrection made it possible, not only that the Kingdom would come to us but also that we would then be able to be animated by the same power that anointed him and come to understand by the same Teacher who taught him.

An added reason for the reserve Jesus showed in speaking about the Spirit might be found in the milieu of first-century Palestine. Bogus pneumatics, people who claimed to be filled with God's Spirit, were not infrequent at that time in that territory. Their bizarre activity and magical powers attracted attention and unstable followers. Thaumaturges, for example, who were workers of spectacular tricks, were not uncommon in Jesus' day. Some of Jesus' reserve about much discussion on the subject of the Spirit could be related to these false pneumatic claims and false claimants and the false expectations that their claques entertained.

d. Spirit-borne Words and Works

Every word that Jesus spoke says something about the
manner of the Spirit's action on man and the relationship
between Jesus and the Spirit of God. The people, those
who were attracted to Jesus as well as those who were
repelled by his words, testified to the fact that when he
spoke, an extraordinary spiritual force was released.
Some chose to trace the origin of this power to Beelzebul
and others to God, but all knew that a power went forth
when he spoke that managed to divide his hearers into
two camps, depending on what they perceived was the
origin of this power. Both in its effect and in its content,
what Jesus said transcended anything the rabbis of his
day were saying. The people noticed, too, that he did
not accommodate or compromise his words. He kept insisting on the truth of what he said, notwithstanding his
audience's incomprehension or rejection of it.

Jesus did not depend on his audience's acceptance of
his words because he was conscious that the source of
what he said was not himself: "The words I say to you I
do not speak as from myself" (Jn. 14:10). Although he
did not belabor it, neither did he hide the source of what
he spoke: "The Spirit of the Lord has been given to me,
for he has anointed me. He has sent me to bring the
good news to the poor . . ." (Lk. 14:18).

If the Spirit was the origin of his words, eternal life
was their consequence. "The words I have spoken to you
are spirit and life" (Jn. 6:63). This means that he was

conscious of teaching only what he learned: "We witness only to what we have seen" (Jn. 3:11). Or: "My word is not my own" (Jn. 4:24). And the effect of receiving the words he spoke? Since they were borne from above, his words effected an eternity in the hearer. "I tell you most solemnly whoever keeps my word will never see death" (Jn. 8:51). The ultimate effect his words would have would be a Kingdom in which God and men were compenetrating presences one to the other. This would come about only when the Spirit was present to men in an indwelling manner as It was to Jesus: "If anyone loves me he will keep my word, and my Father will love him, and *we* shall come to him and make our home with him" (Jn. 14:23).

Those who heard and accepted the words Jesus spoke, sporadically experienced the power of the Spirit that was at the origin of those words, but the personal presence of the Spirit in their hearts in power would be possible only after the moment of Pentecost. Before that moment, however, the words of Jesus were Spirit-borne, life-inviting, and Kingdom-bearing words.

Within the matrix of the words Jesus spoke one can begin to broach the subject of the divinity of Jesus in a new light, one that might be more accessible to our understanding than the two-natures-one-person model of classical Christology. The words that Jesus spoke were not ideas. He was becoming what he was learning and speaking what he was becoming. The Spirit-borne words that he heard were so perfectly received by him that he, a man, was being made over. He was being born again, by his complete receptivity to what the Spirit was speaking to him. What the Spirit of God speaks is reified when it is received. He went from seeing that he was being spoken to, to understanding that he was wholly spoken by the Father. All that he was, was from his Father's affirmation of love. He was what and who his Father said: Word, Son, Beloved One. He did not understand this process as something peculiar to himself (and this is what makes his experience news, news that is good, news that concerns us, the only news we cannot afford to be ignorant of), since he recommends that Nicodemus also "must be born from above . . . born of the Spirit" (Jn. 3:7–8).

In the course of time Jesus knew that he was loved before all else and all others. He realized he was first in his Father's eyes: "in the beginning was the Word," and he came to experience in his person the presence of God as his own Father: "and the Word was with God." And at some point in his life he knew something he never dared to tell anyone, something that only the Spirit could eventually teach men when time had provided a sufficient cushion for them to accept what must have made Jesus gasp when he saw the truth: "and the Word was God."

By the words he spoke in his public ministry, therefore, Jesus was not intending to traffic in ideas or concepts or analyses. Not even ideals. The words he spoke were aimed at the hearts of his hearers, and they were either accepted or rejected there, not in their intellects. The whole person, at the level of affectivity, was being invited to respond to the Spirit-borne words of Jesus. The Kingdom that Jesus announced and that the Spirit would

bring was to be interpersonal, not an intermental Kingdom of philosophical unanimity. The Spirit's activity was
directed at building a Kingdom that was to be an inter-
penetration of personal presences of love centered on the
primordial relationship of love between Father and Son
in the Spirit.

Jesus' words were rejected because there already was
a presence moving freely in many of his hearers' hearts.
"You are unable to understand my language," Jesus insisted, because "the devil is your father . . . [and he is]
the father of lies" (Jn. 8:43–44). They had been born
again, but it was not "from above." The presence of their
father became palpable by their attitudes toward Jesus
and his words. It grieved him that they "have shown
they prefer darkness to the light because their deeds were
evil" (Jn. 3:19).

Not only his words, but also his works were accompanied by a release of power that invited the uncertain
onlooker to make an ultimate decision about him. He intended that his works be signs pointing beyond himself
to a Power that being a simple Nazarene would not explain, and a mere son of Mary and Joseph could never
have imagined, much less performed. These works of his
always brought wholeness to all levels of incomplete existence, whether of soul or body, wind or sea, life or
death.

Of all the works that Jesus did, the ones that seemed
to provoke the strongest reaction, were his acts of exorcism. Each conquest or binding of an evil spirit was a
sign to the people that he enjoyed a power in the world
of spirits. "If it is through the Spirit of God that I cast out

WHEN YOU
RETURN FROM
THE   ALTAR,
BRING   NOT
THE   ASHES
BUT
THE FIRE.

erffert - Pd.in Italy

kers, "then know that the
n you" (Mt. 12:28). Some
uish evil spirits as inspired
man casts out devils only
24). Knowing how irre-
this constituted their final
sbelieved his words and
empowered by the spirit
with the onlookers. Would
up his own kingdom and
he enjoyed before the ad-
an act at cross purposes to
lated and divide himself?
a strong man's house and
as tied up the strong man
er that is superior. "But I
r very eyes," Jesus points
rites the bystander to be-
power over evil spirits was

in fact, is an act of con-
had fallen under the sway
of Satan. From the first moment of his ministry, by having the Spirit posit him in the natural habitat of the
demons, the wilderness, the evangelists are informing us
that the nature of his ministry is a confrontation between
the Spirit of God, which he possesses, and the evil spirit,
which possesses or deceives the people of Israel. His
words show the people the lies they have bought and
the truth they should know; his works show them the
new creation that is to come about through him; and

23

his power over the demonic shows them that the level on which the battle is joined is ultimately one between the Spirit of God and evil. This was the reason why they had to put him to death. What he had to say about himself and his Father and what he saw in their hearts and accused them of being, children of the father of lies, constituted a nonnegotiable confrontation.

The crucifixion, death, and resurrection of Jesus could be viewed as the final resolution of the dramatic power struggle that had been going on in the spirit world. By placing himself in the hands of evil men, he freely assumed all the evil the servant was supposed to expiate. His death, accomplished by means of the "eternal Spirit" (Heb. 9:14), was the ultimate act of exorcism, the act to which all subsequent conquests of the power of evil would have recourse for their efficacy. With the reign of Satan broken, the Spirit would be released and sent into the hearts of men. And with the coming of the Spirit, the reign of God began in other men.

Neither in Jesus nor in us does the Spirit appear to produce a Spirit-consciousness. On the other hand, every word that Jesus spoke was accompanied by an anointing that confirmed him in his belief that its source was the Spirit. And every work he performed was accompanied by a power that confirmed him in his conviction that the Spirit's presence to him was an abiding one. The Spirit was like a pledge to him that his trust of his Father was warranted. The indwelling of the Spirit was like a down payment that guaranteed him that the way he was going and the life he was living would result in an ultimate victory for him and a violent upheaval in the spirit world.

He found little confirmation of his mission, on the other hand, in the reactions of men to his words and his works.

For Christians, too, the Spirit is more evident in the reflexive moment, as confirmatory, than as a presence of which we are conscious. The Spirit in our lives is a down payment, assuring us that what has begun in us will be brought to final successful completion. The Spirit, present in power either in words spoken or in works performed, is a pledge that one is heir to the riches that have been accruing since the first promise made to Abraham. The Spirit's power is the assurance to us that the "not yet" that we await has already begun in us.

e. The Spirit and the Baptism of Jesus

Every line of the Gospels takes on a deeper meaning when it is heard as something that was learned by Jesus or by the community of believers from the Spirit. In the case of Jesus, these lines speak of things that Jesus learned about himself, his Father, the meaning of his life and ours. In the case of the community, these lines speak of things the Spirit was teaching it about Jesus. The subsequent Christological tradition, to which we are all heirs, is rich insofar as it is a product of that which the Spirit has taught about Jesus and impoverished to the extent that it has excogitated an understanding of Christ in isolation from the Spirit. The following is an understanding of two of the mysteries of the life of Jesus of Nazareth, written to exemplify how our understanding of him could be enriched if we perceive his dependence on and association with the Spirit. A Jesus perceived in isolation from the Spirit produces only the memory of a remote figure we have to pedestalize to praise.

Jesus' baptism in the river Jordan reveals more about the relationship between Jesus and Yahweh than his birth in Bethlehem. And the accounts by the four evangelists of his submission to the baptism of John bring together the ascending, or human, and descending, or divine, elements in the personality of Jesus more harmoniously than the Christologies developed by the theologians. The mystery of his person remains, of course, as it does with every person. But much of the obscurantism about Jesus that the infancy narratives and theological treatises contain disappears once we have scrutinized this event more closely.

Jesus was about thirty years old when his public life began. By approaching John at the beginning of it, Jesus is saying something about himself, the Law and the Spirit. John baptized Jesus reluctantly. He complied only because Jesus insisted that "it is fitting that we should, in this way, do all that righteousness demands" (Mt. 3:15). And what did righteousness demand? That every means of attaining union with God that the Law offered should be made use of, including, finally, the radical repentance for one's sins that John preached, which was symbolized by one's immersion in the river Jordan.

So Jesus went down into the river to be cleansed because he, too, was a man, and so it was fitting. His submission to John's baptism tells us something about the self-understanding Jesus had developed. He is saying that the self-awareness he has already come to, though it might leave him alone, will not set him outside of the condition men find themselves in. From the outset, Jesus wanted John to know that his realization of being chosen by God did not mean that he saw his lot as different from ours or that his fidelity was automatic. Jesus was so ordinary, in fact, that John appears subsequently to have had misgivings about him. John (perhaps in prison at this time), summoning two of his own disciples, sent them to the Lord to ask, "Are you the one who is to come, or must we wait for someone else?" (Jn. 7:19).

The ministrations of one whose beginnings were similarly marked with special signs apparently were of considerable importance to Jesus. He would have heard about John from his own mother, that he had leaped in Elizabeth's womb when Mary visited her. Though she was described at that moment as "filled with the Holy Spirit" (Lk. 1:42), John himself is not so described then or later. Spoken of glowingly by Jesus, John is nevertheless only a precursor of the new era of the Spirit, not a member of it. "The least in the Kingdom of heaven is greater than he is" (Mt. 11:11). John was only an adumbration of that which was to come, a gateway Jesus insisted on acknowledging and passing through.

Jesus' descent into the water symbolized an end of something both for himself and for Israel, and his emergence from the Jordan signaled the beginning of a new era, the final epoch in the history of salvation. (He would not have had to know then that these were the dimensions of his action; the same Spirit that led him to do this would lead others, especially the apostles and the evangelists, to comprehend these dimensions.) Jesus was beginning a new exodus out of the bondage that the Law had become. He himself had lived a fully observant life according to the Law; he was the best that religious Israel could produce. Because he had fulfilled "all righteousness" according to the Law, in him the Law could be transcended. The new era was in continuity with the Law's way of effecting union with God, but it would be transcended by a union that was relational and filial.

So much for the event in general. Each of the evangelists adds something unique to our understanding of Jesus' baptism. Mark treats the vision that opens up as Jesus emerges from the water as something that only Jesus perceives. "You are my Son, the Beloved; my favor rests on you." (Mk. 1:11). This becomes significant when we realize that Mark has no Infancy narratives as Matthew and Luke have. The scene at the river Jordan serves the purposes for which the other synoptic Gospels include a Nativity account. It adequately conveys the mystery of his person both to Jesus, as confirmation, and to the reader, as introduction to the Christ of Mark. There is no angel Gabriel and no Virgin Mary, but only the theophany of the Father proclaiming Jesus of Nazareth His Son, fully loved by Him. The descent of the Spirit of God upon him makes his person the locus of the Divine Plenitude and is the sign to the son of his Father's love of him.

Matthew, on the other hand, handles the event as something that unfolds before the eyes of men. Mark's "You are . . ." becomes "*This* is my Son, the Beloved; my favor rests on him" (Mt. 3:17). It is the Trinity's first manifestation in time! That is not to say that God is not

eternally triune, but that we only know Him to be such through the latticelike medium of successive moments in time, the first of which, as suggested in Matthew, is the baptism of Jesus. The mystery of the Trinity and of Jesus must be approached pneumatologically, i.e. traced to the Holy Spirit and to the role It plays in the Godhead itself. The Spirit must be seen in some way as the source of this union between Father and Son. The spacial imagery "descending" and "coming down on him" of the Spirit in the symbol of a dove suggests as much.

Luke's handling of the account of Jesus' baptism is also unique in some respects. John the Baptist is already off the scene in this account, shut up in prison, when Jesus is baptized. John's ministry had created a feeling of expectancy among the people. He had led them to believe that someone who "will baptize you with the Holy Spirit and fire," unlike his baptism which was only with water, was about to come. Luke wants nothing to clutter the account of Jesus receiving the Spirit. Even his baptism is relegated to the position of a mere occasion. It is while Jesus is at prayer, therefore, after his baptism, that the heavens open and the "Holy Spirit descended on him in bodily shape, like a dove" (Lk. 3:22). The whole incident, in fact, is treated as a prefiguration of Pentecost. In the first instance, Jesus received the Spirit; in the second, he sent It. Prayer precedes the descent in both cases, Jesus' and the community's. Pentecost completes that which began at Jesus' baptism so that Jesus becomes not only the recipient but also the bearer of the Spirit.

John's Gospel does not contain a baptismal episode, strictly speaking, but assumes the reader's familiarity with the Synoptics' accounts. When Jesus approaches John the Baptist on the far side of the Jordan where John was baptizing, John is quick to bear witness to what he understood about the person of Jesus. The evangelist has the Baptist exalt him as one who ranks "before me because he existed before me." He hints that Jesus will be the Servant of Yahweh inasmuch as he names him the "Lamb of God" who will suffer for men's sins. The fourth evangelist has his own theological reason for making the Baptist an explicit witness to the identity of Jesus at the moment of Jesus' baptism. His account, therefore, has John pointedly declare: "I saw the Spirit coming down on him from heaven like a dove and resting on him. I did not know him myself, but he who sent me to baptize with water had said to me, 'The man on whom you see the Spirit come down and rest is the one who is going to baptize with the Holy Spirit.' Yes, I have seen and I am the witness that he is the Chosen One of God" (Jn. 1:32–34).

The Baptist is anticipating and introducing the Johanine Book of Signs, which is to follow, in which the glory of Jesus would be seen by those who believed in him. The Baptist is indicating that the source of this glory is the special relationship between Jesus and the Spirit. The sign to John that Jesus was the Chosen One of God was the Spirit's descent upon Jesus. Before the son would glorify his Father by every act of fidelity, the Father would glorify his son by imparting to him the gift of the Spirit. Before Jesus is raised from the pit of death and "proclaimed Son of God in all his power" (Rom. 1:14), he is raised from the water and given the pledge of the

Spirit. Before he is seated at the right hand of the Father and declared Lord, he showed himself our brother, one of us. His sonship was something that was realized fully only when he "offered himself as the perfect sacrifice to God through [or by means of] the Eternal Spirit" (Heb. 9:14).

Each evangelist, therefore, has his own unique way of handling the event as part of the way he develops his own distinctive Christology. The Church has taken their respective understandings of the person of Jesus as no less the work of the Spirit than was Jesus' own understanding of himself. These distinctive Christologies developed in and through the communities that the evangelists visited or were members of. The special charismatic gift of evangelist assumed and depended on the many other gifts in the communities of Christians, each one of which was able to contribute to a further understanding of Christ.

It might even be alleged that, if these accounts were merely carbon copies of one another, that in itself would be a proof that the Spirit had not inspired them. As will be shown later, the work of the Spirit since the Resurrection has been to increase men's understanding and praise of Jesus. The world could not contain the books that could be written about the significance of the life and work of Jesus if the Spirit was their co-author. The mere repetition of another's understanding of Jesus hints at the absence of the Spirit, the same way that parroting the praises one has heard is not the same as praising. Each Christian is, willy-nilly, the bearer of a Christology. He will be a letter written by the Spirit or he will be a carbon copy of what he has heard. If the latter, it will suggest that Jesus used to be and the Spirit never arrived.

Each new understanding of an event in the life of Jesus requires a kind of descent of the Spirit in order for it to be heard from inside the heart. The reader may find it more profitable to begin his quest for a new understanding of the person of Jesus Christ from the moment of his baptism in the river Jordan than from the nativity narratives.

Piecing together the hints contained in each of the four evangelists, it seems that the Genesis account of creation would be an accurate backdrop in which to situate Jesus' baptism. Its full meaning might be construed thus: In the beginning God created the heavens and the earth. But the earth proved to be a formless void, and there was darkness over the deep. God's Spirit hovered over the waters and called forth from the deep one who was light. This man emerged from the formless void, the first born from the darkness. God willed that all perfection would be found in him and that all things in heaven and on earth would be reconciled through him. So the flesh was made Word and the Word was with God and the Word was God, dwelling among us. All who accept the light that he is have life in him. To each he gives the power to become a child of God, the same power that enabled him to see that he was the Beloved Son of the Father. In the new creation, which begins with him and has its existence through him, only children unaccompanied by adults will be admitted. The passage from the formless void into the new creation is presided over and made possible by the Spirit of God, sent now by the

understanding of Jesus as one of us and see in the
Synoptics' temptation accounts the three major temptations that persisted throughout his public life. The devil
suggests that Jesus use his power as "the Son of God" to
do the bidding of the people, to give them the bread they
think they want rather than the bread Jesus knows they
need. How difficult it must have been for Jesus to resist
the temptation to be a wonder-worker, one who turned
stones into loaves, because that is what the people
would warm to. What the people needed, however, was to
know what Jesus knew about himself, that his own person
was the bread that the Father would give to men to feed
them. To settle for working wonders rather than being
the food of eternal life for them, was his temptation.

Another temptation was to perform the once-and-for-
all sign for them, the subject of a spectacular display, such
as hurling himself from the parapet of the Temple so that
all could be compelled into believing him. This was a
temptation to circumvent the human, to have angels
rather than cloddish fishermen and tax collectors as his
supporting cast, to have the kingdom come in a flash rather
than in seed, a spectacular epiphany rather than a growing process. He distinctly chose instead to be the sign
that Jonah was, one who was belched forth from the
depths, having undergone all the trials that man is heir
to, rather than to be a glorious figure pasted onto the
human order of things to pander to its need for an object
of awe.

These were subtle temptations, not blatant ones. The
third temptation, that he will receive all the kingdoms
of the world if he will worship Satan, sounds more crass

than it could possibly have been. Jesus' answer to Satan, "You must worship the Lord your God, and serve him alone" (Mt. 4:10), is some indication of the nature of the temptation. He knew that once he removed his eye from the glory and praise of the Father, many things could be justified as serving the mission for which he was sent. The kingdom that he preached would then become something of this world, and the execution of his mission, a way of serving himself. If the son did not seek to glorify the Father, he would seek to glorify himself.

The Spirit is described as leading Jesus into the desert in order that he be tempted, in order that he see these subtle perversions of his person and mission that would be suggested to him throughout his ministry. He was free to succumb to them or to resist them; otherwise our redemption has been won at the price of coercion. The fact that he did not compromise his person or pervert his mission and accomplished the work for which he was sent gives us reason to praise him. He did not cease to be like us in all things except that he did not sin. A Jesus who could not sin is pedestalized; a Jesus who did not sin can be praised.

Once again it is the Spirit that teaches him what he had to learn: the difference between being a sign and being a spectacle; between pointing to himself and witnessing to the Father; between redeeming the human by raising it up and escaping from the human by flight into spiritualism; between powers used for their own sake and those used for the sake of the Kingdom.

But before we could see his glory, he had another baptism to undergo. Before he is proclaimed son of God in power, he must undertake the task of servant. To become the light that all of us could see, he had to be reimmersed in the formless void that is death.

It is quite possible that the first hint he had about how his mission was to be accomplished, took place at the moment of his baptism as he emerged from the waters of the river Jordan, and heard the voice from heaven proclaim: "This is my son, the Beloved; my favor rests on him" (Mt. 3:17). He would have been sufficiently familiar with the resemblance between those words and the overture to the four servant songs of Isaiah to be able to see the shape of what lay ahead of him.

Isaiah 42:1 has Yahweh declare: "Here is my servant whom I uphold, my chosen one in whom my soul delights. I have endowed him with my spirit that he may bring true justice to the nations." Knowledge that he is to take on the role of servant now begins to intertwine with the realization that he is son and Messiah.

The other possibility, of course, is that this is something that the Spirit is suggesting to the evangelists, who use the occasion of Jesus' baptism to begin the theme of Jesus as the Servant of Yahweh. In either case, the Spirit is teaching us what It taught Jesus about himself. After that he came to understand that the scope of his mission could be glimpsed in the four Servant Songs of Isaiah. He makes allusions to them throughout his public ministry, which suggests what he was culling from them in his own personal ponderings.

In the course of his public life, there would be innumerable occasions for Jesus to be confirmed in his being called to fulfill the Servant's role. Though innocent, he was treated as if he were evil. Though gentle and giving no cause for ill treatment, he is dealt with harshly. Several times he finds greater belief in those who are not of the house of Israel so that the universal scope of the Servant's mission, "to the nations," begins to be glimpsed by Him. The constant accompaniment of the Spirit is something that was promised to the servant and is evident in the power that Jesus' words have over evil spirits and ills of every kind. As a chasm begins to open between himself and those who have grown secure in their Law-bound righteousness, he realizes that there is no resolution of it except by his death. A life freely surrendered as a ransom for the many who were in bondage to a false self image and a false image of God was "the baptism I must still receive." Men would not have their sins washed away except in the blood of the lamb, the lamb that the Father was asking him to become.

Many of his sayings reveal a profound paradox about life. His sense of irony would have been heightened because of the addition of the task of servant to his identity as son and Messiah. In order for men to become sons, he, the Son, had to become the servant. In order for the Spirit to come to convince men that they were sons, he, the Son, had to go. For men to be washed of their guilt, they had to become guilty of taking his life. In order for them to hold on to the ineffectual innocence the Law gave them, they plotted the death of the most innocent of men. In order for Jesus to be known as the Son, he had to send to us the same Spirit who led him to the realization that he was the only Son of the Father.

Perhaps there is a moral, too, for Christians in the relationship between the Servant task and sonship. The disciple is not greater than the master, so the Christian who is called to a new identity as son is also summoned to assume the role of servant. But being a servant of others must be done in a spirit of sonship and should increase one's sense of being son. Any service of others that diminishes or puts in jeopardy one's realization that he is son is a disservice to oneself and will eventually become a disservice to those being served.

The function that the Spirit played in teaching Jesus the Father and His Kingdom, the Spirit now plays in teaching us Jesus. In a sense, all we learn from the Spirit is Jesus since "all he tells you will be taken from what is mine; everything the Father has is mine" (Jn. 16:15). Jesus was so perfect a learner that the Spirit confines what he teaches us to the framework of what Jesus said and did, which the Spirit recalls to our minds and illumines in our hearts. To have what we learn from the Spirit confined to what Jesus is, is not very confining at all. In fact, the world could not contain the books that could be written about him were there enough faithful scribes who brought forth from their storehouse both the new things the Spirit would teach and the old things already taught.

From Following Jesus to Being Led by the Spirit of Jesus

Even if one grants, or already appreciates, the profound relationship between Jesus of Nazareth and the Spirit of God, one can legitimately wonder whether this relationship isn't peculiar to Jesus and the Spirit. What does Jesus' relationship to the Spirit tell us about the Spirit in our lives? An attempt to answer this question could be made abstractly or by spelling out a theology of the Holy Spirit for Christian spirituality. This chapter will forego such an approach and will attempt something more concrete, a biographical appreciation of the Spirit in a Christian's life.

The life of Peter, the apostle, is rich in details about the Holy Spirit. The relationship between Jesus and Peter was drastically affected by the Spirit. We propose, therefore, in this chapter to trace Peter's progression from a life of relationship to God through the Law, to a life of relationship to God through Jesus, to a relationship to

Jesus through the Spirit. In this development we can see the beginnings of an answer to the question about what difference the Spirit makes in our own lives. Rather than dealing with ideas or ideals or theories, Peter's experience should be a helpful vehicle for coming to a greater appreciation of the Spirit in our lives.

Why Peter? As recorded in the New Testament, his life is rich in before, during, and after vignettes. The three stages of his interior development—while under the law, during his sojourn with Jesus of Nazareth, and after Pentecost—are capable of replication in all Christians' lives. He exemplifies the extension of the interiority of Jesus to another. Roman Catholics, especially, have focused on and have been hung up about other aspects of the life of Peter that are of less importance than his interior development and what this could teach us about the Spirit's relationship to us.

God intended that there be an extension to others of the Spirit-authored interior drama that took place in Jesus. But it appears that only the first Christian community understood this and yielded to the intended extension. As for the rest of us in the Church, there seems to be only a slight suspicion of how fully pneumatic our lives are meant to be.

The *before Jesus* phase of Peter's religious development will not detain us. The general outlines of the Israel into which Peter was born are familiar enough to us. The Mosaic Law had sufficiently defined the parameters of the life of the people, that a religious upbringing was inevitable for one born in first-century Israel. The saintly coexisted with the charlatans, with all professing their unswerving belief in Yahweh, monotheism, the sacredness of the Law and the Covenant. Though the people of Israel entertained different expectations and images about their God, these did not have a divisive effect in view of their need to stand as one against their common enemy, imperial Rome.

Simon (a Grecized form of the Hebrew name Simeon) was from a small fishing port on the northern shores of the Sea of Galilee. Besides knowing his home town, Bethsaida, and the fact that he was a married man whose occupation was fishing, there is little else the New Testament has recorded about Simon, son of John, before he met Jesus, who was also from Galilee. The only other fact that we can cull about Simon is that he is described as "without learning" (Acts 4:13), not meaning that he was illiterate but that he had not gone to any of the rabbinic schools.

Peter's responses to the invitations of Jesus will be of particular interest to us in this chapter. These give a frame of reference within which one can trace the development of the piety of Simon from the moment Jesus invites him to depart from his nets to the moment when as a Christian another "puts a belt about him" and takes him where "he would not go," to new life via Rome and death.

It should be noted here, before proceeding to particular events, that there will be less concern about actual chronology and situating the events historically or recapturing the actual words, than may suit some readers. The religious and theological understanding of the evangelists will be of more concern to us here than some of the technical points that the exegete and the scholar rightly concern themselves with. While one must always be concerned that one's spiritual sense of the Scriptures is developed with as much of an assist as scholarship can give, it seems that New Testament scholarship, through no fault of its own and without intending to do so, has caused to develop such a timidity among many good Christians that they no longer trust their own spiritual sense of the Scriptures. This is a regrettable state of affairs; literalism was as reprehensible a way of overusing the text as literati-ism, if one can coin such a term, is a way of neglecting the Scriptures. The following is an exercise in rumination that unabashedly suggests things the text does not literally say and, at the same time, does not apologize for using some freedom to say things that scholars have not discovered in the text.

Quite early in the public life of Jesus, Simon showed so instantaneous a willingness to accept the invitation to follow him that the impression of impetuosity is associated with the character of Peter from the beginning, and nothing that he does or says after that disabuses one of that impression. What looks like a blustery exterior masks an inner pliability, something that the Divine Potter would eventually shape and knead into a rock-hard faith in the man whom he trusted enough to follow without reservation, though he could hardly have known why, since Jesus was still an unknown. At first, it seemed merely the strength and attractiveness of Jesus' character that made Peter leave his nets and the only skill he knew.

43

a. Entitling His Discoveries

We can trace something of the progress in the relationship between Jesus and Simon by the different titles Peter and the other disciples give him. Early in the Gospels, their respect for him, a respect bordering on reverence, appears by their addressing him as *Kyrie,* something akin to our Sir. This title sums up their judgment of the man, the authority of his character, their confidence that they can leave the familiar for the unknown, the safe for the uncertain, if that is where he is going.

We soon find another title beginning to be used of him. Rabbi or Teacher, a title used sparingly in Simon's day, becomes a favorite way of addressing him, indicating that they are beginning to be won over by the authority of Jesus' wisdom and understanding. The relationship could have halted at that level, with Jesus the teacher and Simon the learner. Simon could have honored his own special rabbi by telling others throughout the length and breadth of Israel the insights he had learned at his feet. Simon, who came to appreciate the power of the truths Jesus taught, could have ended up believing in his wisdom, with his belief reposing on the truth of what he said rather than in his person.

The relationship of many Christians with Christ has been arrested at this level. Jesus is as powerful as the lessons he teaches and useful insofar as what he has said can make life meaningful. As insight-giver, his person is expendable. Many who are concerned with doctrinal purity unwittingly encourage this superficial level of belief by implying that there is something sacred in doctrinal statement and dogmatic definition existing independently of and disengaged from the person of Jesus.

Simon, fortunately, did not stop there. He needed more than lessons to satisfy him, and he knew it. There is a suggestion of the more that Jesus was becoming for him in another title, which soon became a frequent form of address in the Synoptic Gospels. Master begins to occur frequently in the text, indicating his disciples' appreciation of the power of Jesus' person. It is not a term of servility but of awe. They were witnesses of his power over such things as wind and sea, and evil. These all were subject to his command. Simon saw not only his own mother-in-law brought to health by Jesus, but he also saw the Master heal the lame, the blind, the deaf, and the possessed, at times and in ways that incurred the wrath of the would-be masters of Israel. Although he shows a reverence for the Law, Jesus nevertheless asserts his freedom over this manner of attaining righteousness by subordinating its prescriptions to the needs of people.

What began as a disciple's need to learn, developed into a complete dependence on Simon's part not for the religious truths that Jesus taught but for the truth of the life of Jesus. When many who had followed him departed, having been told that his own flesh and blood would be the food they would need to continue journeying with him, Jesus asked the Twelve: "What about you, do you want to go away too?" (Jn. 6:67). Simon confessed his dependence by asking: Who shall we go to? You have the words that give us eternal life!

Simon had progressed in stages from admiration of the character of the Nazarene, to reverence for his wisdom, to awe at the power he manifested, to a hunger for his life-giving word. Each of these shows a growth in the betweenness that had developed, the deepening degrees of presence that Simon was allowing himself to experience. But each also leaves unanswered, in fact, just provokes *the* question: Who is this man Jesus?

Many had satisfied themselves that they knew the answer. Nazarenes especially had generally used their familiarity with his family to be certain that he was only Mary's and the carpenter Joseph's son. Perhaps they were like many Christians who, having been furnished with categories that sufficiently contained the mystery of the person, use their familiarity with the categories to assume that no further inquiry into the identity of Jesus is necessary. Still others were then and still are content to have the inquiry done for them by someone else, preferably the omnicompetent professional, holy men. They were willing to have their disbelief or faith repose on someone else's conclusions about him rather than their own. And, finally, there were those who clothed Jesus with someone else's identity: He is a prophet, Jeremiah; or a holy man, Elijah; or a guilty memory, John the Baptist.

"But you, who do you say I am?" Jesus asked. Peter was always a step ahead of the others, it seems, in peeling aside the petals that hid the identity of the person of

Jesus. Perhaps it is this capacity of his, this sign of the depth of presence Simon was according Jesus, that constituted his primacy more than anything else. "You are the Christ, the Son of the Living God" (Mt. 16:16). You are the anointed one of God, the one we have awaited for centuries. I confess my belief that you are the Messiah.

Jesus' reaction to Simon's discovery is significant. He does not compliment him for his analysis or his powers of observation, since he knows that Simon has been given to see something through no merits of his own and through no effort on his part. "It was not flesh and blood that revealed this to you but my Father in heaven" (Mt. 16:17). The consequences? "Simon, son of John, you are a happy man." Why? Because this process has not had its origins in your intellect nor will it remain merely knowledge. "It is my Father's will that whoever sees the Son and believes in him shall have eternal life" (Jn. 6:40).

All previous invitations that Jesus had extended to Simon were in function of this moment when he would see and believe that Jesus was the Anointed One chosen by Yahweh to redeem Israel. From this moment on, Simon's following of the man from Nazareth begins to change from an outer to an inner thing. A knowledge of the identity of Jesus begins to transform the identity of the knower. Prior to this, Jesus had been at pains to tell the Twelve about the Kingdom of God, that it was a secret, like a pearl to be discovered, a seed hidden in the ground, leaven in the dough of one's person. What Simon did not know at this moment was that discovery of the identity of Jesus was tantamount to uncovering the secret of the Kingdom. What he did not know at this moment was that the Kingdom had now begun in him. The old self would pass away and a new person, a person born again from above, a person wholly the product of God's ways and will, would emerge. That person would be increasingly penetrated by the presence of Jesus and would be present to him in a fuller and fuller way as the false self evanesced.

It was most likely at this moment, therefore, that Jesus chose a new name for Simon. When better than when he is *in via* to becoming a new person, the true self that God was calling into being? "So now I say to you, you are Peter and on this rock I will build my Church" (Mt. 16:18). And what better name than the one that means "rock"? Anyone who pierces to the heart of the mystery of Jesus Christ becomes one with and of the same stuff as the Cornerstone whom the builders of another kingdom rejected. Peter is the first such discoverer and, consequently, the rock on which subsequent believers' faith will build. Each one who comes to believe in Jesus will, in turn, become himself a rock by reason of his faith, sustaining others and being sustained by their believing. Together with Peter and in union with the Cornerstone they will be as living stones in a living temple whose prayer is an unending praising of the Father of Jesus.

It is not evident from this that subsequent believers are built on the office of Peter. It is clear, however, that insofar as they are believers they are built on and are in continuity with the faith that Peter had. Having made the same discovery Peter made, they become one community, one household of faith with him and in turn with Christ.

Peter's discovery was a signal to Jesus, and a confirmation to him, that the Spirit from whom he had learned his own identity was active in the hearts of others, teaching them who he was and who they were. The titles given him evolved because Jesus' own self-understanding was in the process of becoming. It is a tribute to Peter and his companions that they were so keenly aware of the changes within Jesus' own self-understanding that they witnessed to this development by the names they conferred upon him. By these names they confirmed Jesus himself in the direction the Spirit was leading him. They, in turn, were developing their own understanding of themselves as they were drawn more and more into relationship with him. Hence, observers become followers, followers become disciples, disciples companions, and companions apostles.

It belonged to the Spirit to sow the seeds of eternal life in the hearts of men through the words and works of Jesus. The Spirit's effectiveness could be measured by the developments in understanding that his followers were attaining to about Jesus. Peter's confession of Jesus as the Messiah signaled to Jesus that the final stage of understanding had been arrived at; the shoot was appearing above ground. A short time later, Jesus rejoiced that there were, by then, a number who had perceived his identity, that there were whole fields white and ready for the harvest, as it were. At that moment, Jesus rejoiced at the abundance; at this moment even one delighted him. "Already the reaper is being paid his wages, already he is bringing in grain for eternal life, and thus the sower and reaper rejoice together" (Jn. 4:36).

The New Testament, while emphasizing the necessity

of Baptism for all who would follow Christ Jesus, neglects
to mention whether the apostles themselves submitted to
an explicit baptismal ceremony. The reason for this might
be found in this confession of Peter. He and the other
apostles after him underwent the effects of Christian baptism the moment that he and they discovered the true
identity of Jesus. It is important to note that the discovery
that Jesus was the Anointed One of God involved as
much a choosing as a seeing. It was as much a decision
about the ultimate direction one's loving would go in as
it was a graced insight into the person of Jesus and,
consequently, Peter's confession of faith was a free choice
flowing from both his loving and his knowing. It is not
a loving that comes *from* his affections but *to* his affections. This affectivity is of divine origin and is a constitu-
tive part of the gift of faith. In exercising it one undertakes a passover, leaving the prospect of living in and for
oneself and dying in one's sins, to living an eternal life
in time with all one's loves flowing into or out from the
love of God in Jesus.

Peter's previous religious condition was one in which
his relationship with God was contingent upon and affected by his observance of Law. The Law mediated an
experience of transcendence, but one that was diluted
to the extent that one was incapable of observing the
whole Law. Although it prescribed, Law itself could not
empower one, whereas in the new dispensation the Law
was placed inside a man in the tablets of one's heart. The
Law was now love and the power to love. The religious
condition that this would produce would not be fully appreciated by Peter or the others till after Pentecost. Then

the Spirit would be released in them and they would experience the full flowering of that which had already begun in them.

Jesus forbade his disciples to tell anyone that he was the long-awaited one, the one for whom Israel hungered. In the case of Peter, it is clear that Jesus was wise in his prohibition. Peter was ready for a new degree of understanding and love of Jesus, but he was not yet ready to surrender any of the previous conceptions he had entertained about the Messiah. What the Christ would do and how Peter would relate to him were susceptible of much illusion. Mountains of false expectations had to be removed and hurled into the sea before the still small seed of faith would have the room it needed to grow in the soil of his soul.

The vast difference between the way Peter wanted the seed to grow and the way it would, becomes evident as soon as Jesus explains to him and the rest of the Twelve that he was destined to suffer, be rejected, and be put to death, only to rise again. Peter, adamantly rejecting such ideas, is rebuked by Jesus: "Get behind me, Satan! Because the way you think is not God's way but man's" (Mk. 8:33). Having named God the author of Peter's discovery, Jesus names Satan the author of his own role expectations and the misconceptions he entertains about the Messiah. A sower other than the Spirit had been at work in Peter and throughout Israel, sowing these false ideas, creating false expectations.

Jesus was swift, almost harsh, in putting down Peter's false expectations because they indicated that Peter was not beyond trying to shape the Messiah into his own image of what the Messiah should be. He wanted to follow Christ Jesus in such a way that Jesus would really be following him. He wanted a Kingdom that would extend and build up his own ego and confirm his own designs rather than a Kingdom of God's own making, that would come down from heaven.

It represented a dangerous moment in the ministry and mission of Jesus. Peter could have used his discovery to proclaim a Kingdom that was largely a product of his own mind and an aggrandizement of himself. Instead of following Jesus, the Servant Messiah, he would have followed his own image of a hero-messiah that was a projection of his own self-love.

Even the most precious of gifts, the gift of faith, can be exploited for one's own ends. Ardent professions of faith can camouflage (even to oneself) a posture of soul that seeks to use God rather than serve Him. Peter would gradually begin to see the connection between the little seed of his faith in Jesus that grew inexorably, absorbing all other ideals, ideas, and goals, and the uncompromising attitude Jesus manifested toward those who (either subtly or emboldened by the brazen power of the evil one) sought to have him deny his own self-understanding. Peter would come to see that the power and presence and life that had come to abide in his own heart was going in the same direction as Jesus was, that it was paschal-tending, in other words. The disciple was not different from the master. The seed, like Jesus, had to fall into the ground and die in order to grow. Peter learned that he did not have to make this happen but only let it happen. As the parable about the Kingdom had intimated, this would happen of itself "night and day, while he sleeps, when he is awake, the seed is sprouting and growing; how, he does not know. Of its own accord the land produces first the shoot, then the ear, then the full grain in the ear" (Mk. 4:27–28)—requiring only Peter's Amen, not his effort.

b. The Slow Progress of the Kingdom

Several incidents show how slow was the progress of the Kingdom's growth in Peter. The Transfiguration event, for example, is a moment at which we can take a measurement. Here again we see the impetuosity of Peter. He is ready to take charge before he understands what is going on; in fact, before what is going on before his eyes has reached its climax—Jesus transfigured, proleptically resplendent with the glory that will be revealed. "Lord," he addresses Jesus, "it is good for us to be here." Rather than accept the invitation to ecstasy being extended to him and to James and John, he is overjoyed to find himself in the big leagues with Elijah and Moses. He is proud to have as his own Master one who appears to be on such familiar terms with the elite of Israel's sacred past.

"If you wish, I will make three tents here, one for you, one for Moses, and one for Elijah." Peter was not at ease with this experience of transcendence, and he shows himself suffering from the temple syndrome, the need to containerize the sacred so that he could have recourse to it whenever and however it suited him. He would learn that in the new dispensation he would not be allowed the luxury of a religion of awe, one that wrapped up and left the sacred on tablets or in tabernacles. He was to learn that neither Jesus nor the Father would be content with his awe. They would place "a heart within him" whereby he could praise and proclaim the marvelous deeds that God had worked in him. Emmanuel, God-with-us, did not come to be stared at but to abide with us and within us.

Peter was still speaking when suddenly a bright cloud covered him and James and John with a shadow, and from the cloud there came a voice that said, "This is my Son, the Beloved; he enjoys My favor. Listen to him." Perhaps Peter is being chided for his self-regarding reaction to the moment of Jesus' transfiguration. He is given, at any rate, the precondition of mind and heart that is necessary for the Spirit to teach him what he had to learn: Become Lord-regarding and keep your attention not on yourself but on Jesus. "And when they raised their eyes they saw no one but only Jesus" (Mt. 17:8).

Perhaps an even better measure of the slowness of the growth of the Kingdom in Peter, the best example of the weakness of his faith, is his triple denial of Christ Jesus in the face of the opposition marshaled against him by official Judaism and imperial Rome. Jesus predicted the denial by Peter and the rest. "You will all lose faith in me this night" (Mt. 26:34). Before Peter denied Jesus, he denied that his faith was weak. "Even if all lose faith in you, I will never lose faith." He vigorously protested that he would go to prison or to death for Jesus, so strong was his faith in his own autogenic capacity for action taken on behalf of Christ.

At this stage of his spiritual maturation, he was self-reliant. His loyalty to and affection for Jesus, he was sure, would carry him to the heights of a heroism he foolishly preened himself capable of attaining. Just as "flesh and blood" had not given him the gift to perceive the Messianic identity of the Nazarene, so he would find that the affection he had for Jesus was largely a flesh-and-blood thing that would not sustain or empower him.

If the Good News that is our faith had been arrested at this point in Peter's development and he was the rock on which Christianity pivoted, then our faith would be a Jesus fan club, only as strong as the affections it could elicit for the attractive figure of Jesus and only as coherent as natural devotedness could make it.

Immediately before Jesus' prediction that his own select, inner circle of followers would scatter and their faith in him fail, a dispute broke out among them, according to Luke, as to "which should be reckoned the greater." This is another revealing index of their stage of development and, consequently, of the growth of the seed of faith within them. It is still unclear to them that life in the Kingdom consisted of his empowerment of them, not of their performance on his behalf. Greater or lesser are not Kingdom categories, Jesus would tell them, and they are to have no place among them. They are, in fact, erroneous categories, since each of the gifts is for the service of the community and the exercise of each is essential to the wholeness of the community. "There is a variety of gifts but always the same Spirit," Paul would say; "there are all sorts of service to be done but always the same Lord." As long as they were self-regarding, their own performance and a comparison of themselves with others diverted their attention from the Lord's presence, the Spirit's empowerments, the neighbor's need, and the variety of gifts that had to be received by men to meet those needs.

Jesus turns to Peter at the time of the contentiousness about positions in the Kingdom and exclaims: "Simon, Simon! Satan, you must know, has got his wish to sift you all like wheat; but I have prayed for you, Simon, that your faith may not fail and once you have recovered, you, in your turn, must strengthen your brothers" (Lk. 22: 31-34). We should note, first of all, that Jesus is using Peter's previous name, suggesting that there had been a backsliding, a reversion from the life of the Kingdom in which he was present to God and God was present to him. Satan had momentarily succeeded in becoming the principle of his judgments. Jesus was saying this to Peter: "Satan's wish—and it will be granted—is to shake violently asunder what I have joined together, to return each portion of the dough that I have kneaded together back to its separated condition as so many isolated grains of wheat. Just as I myself will go to my death, so the work that I have done in my followers will go to its death. But it and you will be reconstituted, as I myself will be, rising on the third day. I will then begin to fashion with you a new heaven and a new earth. And the assurance I give you that this setback will only be temporary, the death momentary, is that I have prayed for you to the Father that He will reveal anew to you what will have happened to me and what that means for your presence to Him through me, and my presence to you. I have prayed for this in the Spirit who has made us as one, wedding me to the Father and you to me. What will come from our being scattered, therefore, is a new and deeper unity, one that is bathed in my blood and purified by my self-gift to the Father for you."

When all of this happens, Simon will once again be called Peter and rock, because of Jesus' prayer for him. After he has been purified, and the dross of his self-reliance stripped from him, and his understanding enlightened so that he sees the Messiah had to suffer so as to enter into his glory, then the stuff of his former belief will be reintegrated and he will be rock again. He will then serve others by his believing love of Jesus, not as he has imagined him, but as he was and is. He will then be someone to rely on, someone who can confirm the brethren. The primacy will once again be his because he will be the first to believe in Jesus crucified and risen.

c. The Trek After a "Ghost"

Peter must have thought at times that there was something absurd about his companionship with Jesus, as if it were a trek after a ghost over a path as insecure as water. One paradigmatic event, mentioned only by Matthew, sums up the near absurdity of this whole phase of Peter's relationship with Jesus. Whether such an incident actually took place or whether it took place in the way in which it is narrated, is of much less concern to us than the fact that the Evangelist records, for our reflection, a perfect depiction of the interior dispositions of Peter vis-à-vis Jesus before Pentecost.

The incident that epitomizes this phase of Peter's life is described as taking place after Jesus had withdrawn from the company of his disciples to go up to the mountain to pray. He sent them on ahead of him in their boat. A little before dawn he caught up with them "and when the disciples saw him walking on the lake they were terrified" (Mt. 14:26). Many exegetes prefer to place this pericope among the post-Resurrection and pre-Pentecost incidents rather than in the public ministry of Jesus, where Matthew situates it. Agreeing with the exegetical reasons for this, the incident certainly would be more intelligible in a post-Resurrection context, since Jesus is perceived as a "ghost" by those in the boat, an unsurprising perception of one who has been crucified and yet has risen from the dead.

Peter saw more than a ghost, or hoped to anyway. "Lord, if it is you, tell me to come to you across the water." Peter was anticipating, a bit prematurely as it turns out, a time when what Jesus had promised would be realized. "Whoever believes in me will perform the same works as I do myself, he will perform even greater works" (Jn. 14:12). Given Pentecost, this would be true; then he would not imitate the Lord by a reduplication of the externals of his actions but by personally appropriating the same power that animated Jesus.

There is probably more of symbol than historical concern in the narrative. Peter had left his bark to accompany Jesus on the shore and, in the next three years, throughout the length and breadth of Palestine. He would one day leave his own native shores to speak of Jesus in foreign lands. At this moment, however, he perceives the winds that would carry him there as a hostile force. "As soon as he felt the force of the wind, he took fright and began to sink." Jesus, by way of contrast to Peter and the disciples, who also found the wind inimical to their progress, is transported by this same wind across the waves. It was as if the Spirit had become so predominant in him because of his prayer and trust of his Father and his free acceptance of his own death that he was raised above the limitations of matter.

Perhaps the incident is showing Peter and his companions the effect there will be even on their physical persons when the gift of the Spirit, which he is to send to them, will be received by them. Their faith in him will become so powerful, given the Spirit, that their bodies will be instruments of and subordinate to their own spirits. In the Spirit, their interiority will suffuse their external, corporeal existence, as his is doing here. The word spoken within them then would be heard so perfectly that even their bodies would speak and be wordless witnesses of the power of the Spirit and of Him Who sent this Gift.

What was spectacular in Jesus' walking on the water was to be ordinary when those who had faith in him would be similarly empowered. When the Spirit was received by them, they too would be raised, not above and outside of their bodies—a hope that the dualisms of history usually held out for their adherents—but to a condition in which their physical beings would be moved by the dictates and determinations of the inner self. The Spirit was not to be the antithesis of or inimical to the flesh but rather the principle of its activities. Or so it was intended. The varying forms of angelism and Manichaeism in the course of Christian history that would have man good only to the extent that he made himself "spiritual" or saw himself bodiless, have distorted the realism of Christianity. When the body and the outer senses are in control of the spirit and the inner sensibilities, the results are evident. Paul describes them as "fornication, gross indecency and sexual irresponsibility." Since interpersonal presence is impossible then, relationship is simulated. And if exploitation of others is not the result of a life in which the senses are dominant and imperious, then contentiousness with others usually is. "Feuds and wrangling, jealousy, bad temper and quarrels; disagreements, factions, envy; drunkenness, orgies and similar things" (Gal. 5:19-21) break out when self-indulgence, "the opposite of the Spirit" is the principle of one's activity.

When "the Spirit is our life," however, the body is not disparaged but is rather the locus that magnifies the presence of God-with-us. "What the Spirit brings is very different: love, joy, peace, patience, kindness, goodness, trustfulness, gentleness and self-control" (Gal. 5:22).

The fact that the wind was depicted as a hostile force for the disciples in their rowing and to Peter in his attempt at imitating his Master is susceptible of another interpretation than a merely physical one. It hints at the pre-Pentecost condition of their spirits. The wind (*pneuma* in Greek means either wind or spirit) accompanies, surrounds, and propels the Risen Christ. It comes with his coming, and joining him or being joined with him is impossible now except in and through the power of the Spirit. At this moment the disciples were still relying on their own powers to get to the other side, and Peter was relying on the power of his own intention to get him to Jesus. They were all unsuccessful.

Peter, on his own initiative, induced an invitation from Jesus to come to him on the water. He would learn the near futility of following Jesus on the basis of his own affection, intention, and power. Hence the need for emergency measures in this situation. "Jesus put out his hand at once and held him. 'Man of little faith,' he said, 'why did you doubt?'" (Mt. 14:31–32). Simply willing it would not make the following of the Risen One possible. One must face the issue of the *Pneuma*, the Spirit, if following the Risen One is to be anything more than a memory or a velleity.

There seems to be another level of significance to this passage. It suggests that there are two ways of following the Risen Lord, one from the boat and another, with him, on the waves. There are, at least, two possible ways for a Christian to live his life. In the first way, he can enjoy the relative security of bark, numbers, and practice, although he might have to cope with the pervasive feeling that "we are not really getting very far." Or one can accompany Jesus on the waves and resign oneself to the precarious, almost capricious, it seems, element of the Spirit which, like the wind, "blows wherever it pleases." This second option puts one outside the social confirmation that one's milieu can provide. One's sole support is then much more starkly faith in the person of Christ Jesus. A life of complete faith propels one to live not by his own ideas, impulses, or abilities, but by the leadings of the Spirit that have much the same ebb and flow and unpredictability that wind and waves do.

Boat-huggers, by contrast, are happier with something definite to do and some assurance that eventually the bark will posit them up on the shores of eternity. "Master, what good deed must I do to possess eternal life?" But wave-walkers, by contrast, are dissatisfied with distance, and desire the immediacy of Jesus' risen presence. Peter would soon be invited into this presence. Jesus would call him from the religious condition of routinized, discrete acts that had to be done, and done in such a way that the actor was over against the object of his belief because of the complete otherness of Jesus as risen. The ultimate singularity of each person, even the Risen Lord, is something that only the Spirit can reverse. By giving him this Gift, Jesus would call him from the poverty of a religion of discrete acts to a rich relationship of mutual presence. But the price Peter would be asked to pay would be to give up his own footing, his rootedness in himself alone.

"Man of little faith, why did you doubt?" Jesus' words could mean something more than criticism of Peter for his taking his eyes off of him and putting them on the sea into which he was sinking or on the wind that was about to sweep him off his feet. Perhaps "little" rather describes the slight amount of faith one can be expected to have in the pre-Pentecost condition of religious development. The doubt for which he is chided, in that case, would be his attempted following of the Risen Christ by inducing an invitation from him to join him prematurely on the water. When the Spirit came, the power of Peter's faith, as also the faith of the other followers of Jesus, would be dramatically deepened. Once the Spirit is sent into their hearts, then "little faith" will describe those who must cling to the social confirmation that the bark affords. The natural milieu for the rest will be on the water and the waves—in the wind.

d. Relationship with the Risen One

On the shores of the Sea of Tiberias Peter was taught the meaning of service of his brothers and sisters in the new Kingdom. He had by this time come through the traumatic experience of being handed over into the power of Satan. He had seen the Lord risen as predicted. And, in John's Gospel, where this particular pericope is found, the Holy Spirit has been already breathed upon him and the others. "As the Father has sent me, so am I sending you. After saying this he breathed on them and said: Receive the Holy Spirit" (Jn. 20:21–22). Peter is just beginning, therefore, the third, or Pentecost, phase of his relationship with Jesus. In it, he is, by his own choice, being handed over to the power of the Spirit that has been breathed into him by Jesus. Because he yields to it, the Spirit brings him into the presence of the Risen Jesus. Jesus appears on the shore while Peter and the others are attempting to catch fish, which they manage to do only because, at his word, they let down the net.

Like the previous passage, this one too has several levels of meaning, the least important of which is the historical, and the most significant of which is the symbolic. For example, the net that Peter hauls ashore is found to have 153 fish, a number St. Jerome tells us, which neatly corresponds to the number of every species of fish known by the ancient zoologists contemporary with John the Evangelist. If this is so, the author would be saying in a quaint way how universally effective the mission of Peter and the apostles would be, given the presence of their Risen Lord.

The picture of the disciples hauling the net ashore filled with every kind of fish suggests, then, that the Kingdom has already begun now that the Spirit has been received by the followers of Jesus. The author might have had Matt. 13:47–48 in mind: "The Kingdom of heaven is like a dragnet cast into the sea that brings in a haul of all kinds. When it is full the fishermen haul it ashore. . . ." The Apostles are now living in Kingdom times, doing Kingdom things, Peter first and foremost. Jesus is the dispenser now of the Spirit-Gift. "This was the third time that Jesus showed himself to the disciples after rising from the dead" (Jn. 21:14). With breakfast over, Jesus probes, testing the effects on the character of Peter of the Spirit's coming in power. "Simon, son of John, do you love me more than these others do?" Is he still comparing himself to others, Jesus wondered? Relying on his own resources and powers? Is the base from which he lives and from which his actions spring his affection for (and, therefore, possibly disaffection for) me and others? Before sending the Spirit, Jesus left them with the commandment to love one another as he had loved them. With the sending of the Spirit, love was to be not a commandment to be observed but a description of the way they lived with one another. The key test of the presence of the Spirit is love. So before sharing with Peter and after Peter with the others his own shepherd role in the Kingdom, Jesus had to be sure that the new principle of Peter's actions, the Spirit of Love, had been received by Peter. Peter assures him it had. "Yes, Lord, you know I love you." And Jesus, now assured, says, "Feed my lambs." One would have thought, Peter certainly did, that with this awesome responsibility having been conferred upon him, Jesus would have had some advice about the pasturing of the sheep and lambs he had given his life for. But this is not the case. He reverts to the same question not once but twice more.

Many find in the threefold questioning of Peter's love for Jesus a redressing of the triple denial Peter had been guilty of during the Passion. Although such an interpretation is quite plausible, it is also true that Jesus is teaching Peter the most important thing he has to know to perform on his behalf the role of Shepherd of his sheep.

Peter had to be asked three times about his love of Jesus perhaps because being a practical man he probably was focusing on the tangible, the manner, the efforts that would have to be made to do the work of pasturing the lambs and sheep. But what Jesus is teaching him by his repeated questioning is that the lambs and sheep will be fed, not by Peter's concern for them nor by his service of them as such but by his believing love of Christ Jesus.

He had to be asked three times in order to finally focus on what it was that would be service Kingdom-style. He is not being commanded to love, he is being asked whether he does. To the degree that he does, the sheep are led, the lambs are fed. The degree of Jesus' presence to him and his presence to Jesus is the way the sheepfold will be safe and the sheep pastured. This illumines the passage in Ezekiel about the manner and immediacy of God's presence in the new dispensation. "Thus says the Lord God: I *myself* will look after and tend my sheep. As a shepherd tends his flock . . . so *I* will tend my sheep. I *myself* will pasture them . . . shepherding them rightly" (Ezk. 34:11–16). Jesus is not relinquishing his function to Peter and the others. He is describing the manner of his presence. Through Peter's love of him and others' love of him, a flock would be gathered and pastured.

The lesson is then underscored by the subsequent passage. After conferring upon Peter for a third time the Shepherd responsibility, Jesus continues: "I tell you most solemnly, when you were young you put on your own belt and walked where you liked; but when you grow old you will stretch out your hands and somebody else will put a belt round you and take you where you would rather not go" (v. 18). The mysterious "somebody else" who would take him, lead him where he would rather not go was, of course, the Spirit. As Peter freely chose his Lord, he was bound to him as if their presence to one another was entwined by a belt fastened by the Spirit. In a sense it was a death for Peter. "In these words [Jesus] indicated the kind of death by which Peter would give glory to God. After this he said, 'Follow me'" (v. 19).

Peter's death was to be a gradual thing, a question of decreasing while he increased. He was to die to doing his own thing, even his most impetuously generous or religiously inspired thing, so that the Shepherd through the Spirit could do his thing in him. Under the leading of the Spirit he would be led away from a service of others that was self-serving, to relationship with others that was both a loving and a witnessing to the love by which he himself was loved. The ever-present proof of Jesus' love of him was his gift to him of the Spirit of Love. It was not a gift that was to be peculiarly his any more than the commission to nourish another by means of his love was a commission to him alone or to the apostles. Jesus' proof of his love was the gift of the Spirit; the evidence that It was received was to appear in the quality of relationships that obtained between members of the community.

In this third or Pentecost phase of their relationship, we find Peter and the disciples conferring on Jesus the name that they could not have called him during his sojourn with them since it would have been untrue of him then, even blasphemous. But once he was raised from death and elevated above every order of created being, then he was given by his Father the name that God alone was called: Lord. (*Kyrious* is the Greek way of rendering the two Hebrew names for God, YHWH and Adonai.)

The Spirit began to teach Peter and the others the "all things" that Jesus promised they would learn by telling them their Master's new name, Lord, and the new relationship he had toward them. "No one can say Jesus is Lord except in the Holy Spirit" (I Cor. 12:3). The fact that Jesus himself now enjoyed the title heretofore reserved for God Himself, helped to launch a process of reflection that would eventually culminate in the understanding that Jesus from Nazareth was himself "God from God, light from light, true God from true God, begotten not made, one in being with the Father by whom all things were made" (Nicene Creed).

III

The Personality of the Holy Spirit

It would seem that there is a conspiracy of silence among Christians about the personality of the Holy Spirit. Admittedly, there have been moments in our religious history when there has been much talk about what the Spirit does. We are presently going through one of these periods. But what the Spirit is like, who the Spirit is, the characteristics of the Person of the Spirit, these questions have received such scant attention from hierarchs and theologians that one would have almost to suspect a pact several thousand years old to ignore the subject. It is as if our inclusion of the Holy Spirit in our doxologies were sufficient and an excuse for the virtual exclusion of the Spirit from our formal and informal animadversions in the Church.

There are probably many reasons for the silence, but the main one should be traced to the Spirit Itself. It seems that a major characteristic of the Spirit's personality is transparency. The Spirit aims at being inconspicuous. In activity It points to the Other, making us aware of Jesus

as our Lord and God as our Father. The nonawareness of
the Spirit's presence, therefore, may be a better proof of
Its activity in the person, group, or community than anything that brings It into explicit attention. Having said
this, however, we must immediately add that there is a
greater need than ever to pursue an inquiry into the
Spirit's personality, notwithstanding the limits that this
tantalizing characteristic of transparency imposes upon
us. Though we have to approach the question obliquely
and from the effects of the Spirit's workings, we must address ourselves to it nonetheless.

The wind will teach us much about the Spirit's personality. If that seems like a preposterous suggestion, con-
sider how often Jesus himself played on the similarities
between the qualities of wind and the characteristics of
the Spirit. "The wind blows wherever it pleases," he observed; for example, "You hear its sound, but you cannot
tell where it comes from or where it is going. That is how
it is with all who are born of the Spirit" (Jn. 3:8).

Even linguistically, there is an invitation to think of the
Spirit as if it were a Divine Wind, since the Hebrew
word *ruah* means both spirit, wind, and breath. The Old
Testament reflections of Yahweh's Chosen People are
enlightening in this respect. They saw Yahweh's own
breath as an instrument for fashioning them. By a fierce
blast of His breath, for example, He parted the seas,
which His people walked through to escape from Egypt.
It was a divinely sent wind that bore the manna and the
quail that fed them as they journeyed to the land of the
promise. And Yahweh's very own Spirit had come to
rest on special individuals while Israel was still in the age

of the prophets. It was the word He breathed into the hearts of His prophets and put on their lips that nurtured His people and shaped their lives according to His designs for them.

When the Divine *Ruah* came, they reflected, it was sent by Him bringing good things as well as chastisements. But it did not remain outside of a man, they came to see, as if it were a mere creature of the environment, an element in the atmosphere. It was breathed into them and became the principle of life in a man. Man became a living being, therefore, by the breath of Yahweh Himself. If He should withdraw His breath (and it never ceased to be His), then a man would die.

Gradually, both the wind He sent as His instrument, the breath He breathed into men, and the force of His own Spirit, which rested on chosen individuals, were conceived less vagrantly and with more precision. In the course of this discernment, Israel did not cease to believe in or withdraw its credence from any of these ways of Divine activity, but became more discriminating about Yahweh's own Spirit. It is conceived of less anthropomorphically, in a way that is increasingly immaterial and prospective. His Spirit becomes primarily something that is to come; It will accompany the person of the Messiah. The Messiah, in turn, will inaugurate a new age in which Yahweh Himself promises: "I will give them a single heart and I will put a new spirit in them" (Ezk. 11:19).

An inspirited Messiah was not to be a momentary eruption of the Divine into the human order or the selection of an individual as a special instrument of God. No, the Messiah himself would inaugurate a new age. Yahweh's own Spirit, was to indwell a people, in that age which was to last not for a moment but for all days, even to the end of time. Needless to say, the monotheism of Judaism did not allow them to conceive of the Spirit of Yahweh as a distinct, divine Personality. So the wind that was heard at Pentecost would not yet be Someone to those who heard It, but a powerful sign nonetheless that what they had so long awaited, had come.

It would do no harm—on the contrary, it would be fruitful—to sense the aptness of the wind as a symbol of the Spirit. The properties of the one are the inferable qualities of the Other. As with both Spirit and wind: it is uncontainable by men, nor can men control it. Men have never been able to reconnoiter its origins nor renegotiate its directions. Though invisible, the wind's effects are palpable. What is not firmly planted and solidly rooted, the wind will overturn.

It can be counted on to be sufficiently present so that men will not be left without shade or shower, thunder or calm; we can enjoy the toil of our labors and the fruit of the earth because of the wind's capacity to bring us variation. And yet this wind is unpredictable, capricious almost. It is pathless in its direction. And in intensity it can be a gale or a zephyr, confined to no one degree by man —wafting and caressing some, uprooting others ruthlessly.

Imagine a planet with too much wind, such as Venus. It would be intolerable for us mortals. And a planet with no wind at all, such as the moon, would be equally inhospitable. Men would not have known the meaning of voyage if they lived in a world without wind. Other

lands, new horizons, cultures other than their own would
have remained foreign to them if the wind had not
caught the sails that men spread out to it. It carried them
to where, under their own power, they could not have
gone. Becalmed, we would have remained primitives.
Even the mightiest of men is dwarfed by the power of the
wind, and the greatest of men would still be the least in
the human species if ours were a world without wind.

The birds of the air seem wiser about it and more
versed in utilizing the wind than humans. They learn
rapidly how to glide with its waftings, and be one with its
playfulness. Soaring would be too strenuous if attempted
under their own power. Ready to alight any moment the
wind stirs them, they live ready to leave, neither sowing
nor reaping nor gathering into barns. And when all is
still and no stirrings come, they seem to know that they
must be careful lest their wings grow heavy. No, an
absence of wind won't last for very long. All of the
properties of wind have something to tell us about the
Spirit and how it comes and works among us.

Jesus taught his followers relatively little about the
Holy Spirit who was to come to them sent by him and
the Father. They did not know the qualities of this new
force nor that it was itself a Divine Person. But the little
he did teach them explicitly, they learned well. He
claimed it would be to their advantage that he should go
in order that the Spirit could come. They had seen with
their own eyes how the winds obeyed him and could
have reasoned that he would not send them anything of
such gale force that they would be capsized by its coming. "Stay in the city then until you are clothed with the

power from on high," he told them. They stayed, and once they received the Power they were spirited not unlike the birds of the air, all the way to the ends of the earth.

As with any analogy, the Spirit as Divine Breath or windlike, enlightens one up to a point, but then, its work done, it breaks down and becomes an ineffective means for contemplating the mystery of the Personality of the Spirit.

a. Descriptive Names for the Spirit

Two of the descriptive names that Jesus uses of the Spirit when speaking to his own followers can bring us a step farther into the mystery of the Spirit. One of these names was Paraclete, according to John the Evangelist. "Parakletos," meaning Paraclete or Advocate, says a good deal both about the Personality of the Spirit and Its relationship to us. By employing a term with legal connotations, Jesus is saying that the Gift he will be sending to his own will give them someone who will argue their case on their behalf with God (and It will suggest to their minds ways of arguing their own case with men) as well as teach, lead, and defend them. Because of this gift there was to be a Divine element dwelling in men. The Divine was now on the human side of an otherwise unbridgeable chasm between men and the wholly Other, God.

The individuality of Jesus, even as Risen Lord, is incommunicable; his Incarnation leaves him himself,

74

unique in his individuality, as any man is, and therefore, over against us, as another always is. But with the sending of the Spirit whose Personhood is not by generation and whose uniqueness is not by way of incarnation, the distance between man and God could be bridged, the process of individuation and, consequently, of separation could be overcome. The eternal procession of the Spirit within the Godhead is by way of Spiration, the theologians tell us. When the Gift is given to men in time It proceeds from the Father and the Son. When It is received the Spirit becomes a Conspirer in a man, with the recipient and the Spirit breathing as one. Because the Spirit is the Spirit of love, the two become as one, as if in a communion. Individuality is not lost, then, or surrendered, but transcended and rooted in the truth. As was the case with Jesus in his relationship with the Father, the unity between the two that the Spirit effects makes each more fully and uniquely himself.

At first, the hearers of Jesus thought the Spirit was to be a Divine Force that they would be enveloped in. Eventually, Christians came to see that the Divine element that Jesus had gifted them with was also God, a distinct Person with qualities and, looked at from the side of time, a history that Jesus Christ did not have and that they had not perceived in the Divine Personality of Yahweh.

Without the Spirit, Jesus would have been to Christians only a model, a goal, a memory, an ideal. But given the personality of the Spirit, Jesus has become Emmanuel, God-with-us. Because of the Spirit, it is possible for the Senders—Jesus and his Father—to join the Sent. "If any-

one loves me he will keep my word, and my Father will
love him, and we shall come to him and make our home
with him" (Jn. 14:23). How can the Spirit, who is God,
come to us, and at the same time make room in us for
God? This question isolates the mystery of the Personality of the Spirit. In other words, we have come to
Mary's question: "How can this come about?" And if the
Gift has come to us, we will be able, not to answer the
question, but to live with the mystery. "Be it done unto
me according to thy word."

Rather than be concerned with knowing the incomprehensible, we must be anxious that we are disposed
to receiving the mystery of the Spirit. We keep the Lord's
word, we obey his command and follow the Way that he
goes and become one with his becoming if we welcome
the One "whom I shall send to you from the Father" (Jn.
15:26). Since the Spirit is our Advocate, It will breathe
with us, pray in us with unceasing groanings, act on our
behalf, enlighten us about who we are, while teaching us
Jesus and the Father. Counseling, consoling, interceding
and pleading for us with God are the other roles that
tradition has attributed to the Spirit.

The other name that Jesus uses of the Spirit is the Spirit
of Truth. This can sound like the Spirit is an idea or the
sender of truths or thoughts to us. Unlike the exchange
of truths that pass between us humans, what the Spirit of
Truth says to us becomes the reality spoken and heard.
The Spirit effects the reality It speaks. Reductively, what
the Spirit always says is love, since that is what God is.
It seems interchangeable and convertible, therefore, for
the Spirit to be called a Spirit of Love or a Spirit of Truth.

When the Spirit comes It touches those to whom It is sent with subsistent Love. It brings men in some way into the actual presence of Love, the Love that exists between Father, Son, and Spirit. Depending on their receptivity, the Spirit empowers men to become the reality they are being touched by: lovers, in other words. Through the Spirit, one's eyes can come to perceive, hesitantly at first, murkily for a long time, but unmistakably, nonetheless, new vistas and undreamed-of panoramas of reality, "for the Spirit reaches the depths of everything, even the depths of God" (I Cor. 2:10). First and foremost what one sees is the truth of his own being in the love that the Father and Son have for him. In and through the Spirit one comes to see who one is. And what one is being led to become, comes into being. The word spoken and heard "will not return to me empty." The truth of one's being loved is the truest thing about one's own identity. From these roots, in the seeds of that truth, one begins to be made wholly new.

What the Spirit *is* within the Godhead, the Spirit *does* among men. Our ordinary Christian speech seems to appreciate this creative power of the Spirit to effect the reality It touches with the reality It is in a way that our minds do not always comprehend. Hence, our favorite way of referring to the Spirit is Holy Spirit. Our speech confesses our realization that It sanctifies what It touches. Its coming cleanses and purifies and makes holy that which It enters and indwells.

There are several other things about the words we use in referring to the Spirit that we should advert to here. It is significant that we refer to Jesus as *our* Lord and

God as *our* Father but never to the Spirit as *our* Spirit. Once again, it seems that our theological sensibilities are sometimes more acute than our ability to articulate them. Although the Spirit is very much on *our* side of the Divine Reality, and given to us to be our Advocate, as we have noted, we seem to have a sense that we are more possessed by the Spirit than possessor of the Spirit. Consequently, we have a sense that *our* Spirit would be an inappropriate expression, even though we feel free to use *our* of both Lord and Father, since they remain wholly other and over against us.

There are several ways, however, in which we could be a little more precise in our Spirit speech. Why should the Spirit be referred to with the pronoun He? It is obvious why Jesus and the Father should be, but there does not seem to be any theological reason for referring to the Spirit with the masculine pronoun—or with the feminine, for that matter. One could argue that since the Holy Spirit is a Person and since we do not have experience of any other person who is not either masculine or feminine, it seems that we should choose one or the other pronoun when speaking of the Spirit. Perhaps, but there is no human person even remotely similar to the Spirit. Before the days of consciousness-raising by feminists, the point probably received little or no attention, but given that attention, we should reflect on what seems more appropriate. My own preference in this work has been to use the neuter pronoun for the One whose artistry is in the area of relationship, making we's where there were only I's before while remaining so inobtrusive as to seem almost transparent.

And, finally, a quibble, or perhaps more than a quibble. I think the use of the phrase "the inspiration of the Holy Spirit" implicitly denies our belief in the reality of the indwelling of the Holy Spirit. "Inspiration" connotes something coming in from out of the blue, rather than up from the depths of my own spirit in union with the Spirit. The word conveys poorly the relationship between the spirit of the person and the indwelling Spirit. The promptings of the Spirit, therefore, would be more accurately called "conspirations," I submit, since what is produced by following them is partly stamped by the Spirit and partly by the human spirit acceding to them.

b. The Spirit's Epiphany in the Event of Pentecost

So much for what we can learn about the Spirit's personality from the Old Testament and Jesus' words as well as our own vocabulary. A whole new horizon of understanding of the Spirit can be found in the event of Pentecost, which was the primary epiphany of the Spirit. The less than evident features of the Spirit's Personality as well as all subsequent comings of the Spirit into the hearts of persons can be illuminated by reflection on this event.

As a background to the mystery of Pentecost, we should call to mind the thirty-seventh chapter of the Book of Ezekiel. It strikingly portrays why the coming of the Spirit and the event of Pentecost was a matter of urgency for man. The prophet Ezekiel is transported, the reader will recall, to an immense valley eerily still and strewn from one end to the other with the bones of men bleached white with death. Yahweh explains to Ezekiel that this is the condition in which He finds His chosen people. If they even knew their plight, they would cry out: "Our bones are dried up, our hope has gone; we are as good as dead" (Ezk. 37:11). Yahweh describes the future event through which these bones shall live. "The Lord Yahweh says this to these bones: I am now going to make the breath enter you, and you will live . . . and you will learn that I am Yahweh" (v. 6). The valley of the dry bones will be transformed into another Eden filled with living things and men fully alive. This will happen, Yahweh prophesies, when "I shall put my spirit in you" (v. 14).

The important thing to note about the scene is the significance of Yahweh's own breath to men who are as inert as bones. Without it their condition is hopeless, they are as desiccated bones bleached with the heat of the unrelenting sun. But one should also note that, with the invasionlike inspiration of His own Spirit into them, they will not experience His Spirit as such. Rather, they will experience themselves as alive and Yahweh as their Lord and their own collective unity, their coming together as one.

"WHEN PENTECOST DAY CAME ROUND, THEY HAD ALL MET IN ONE ROOM, WHEN SUDDENLY THEY HEARD WHAT SOUNDED LIKE A POWERFUL WIND FROM HEAVEN, THE NOISE OF WHICH FILLED THE ENTIRE HOUSE IN WHICH THEY WERE SITTING; AND SOMETHING APPEARED TO THEM THAT SEEMED LIKE TONGUES OF FIRE;

THESE SEPARATED AND CAME TO REST ON THE HEAD OF EACH OF THEM" (Acts 2:1–3).

The monumental event of Pentecost was perceived first as a powerful wind. God's choice of symbol could not have been more apropos, since for centuries, as we have seen, Israel was developing its understanding of Yahweh's Spirit as windlike. Its coming was also perceived as fire. This symbol too had a long history. Yahweh's previous theophanies had usually been engulfed with fire. It was in fire that Yahweh gave His people the Law as their way to Him. It was in fire, pillarlike, that He went before them, leading them out of the wilderness. The fire He cast upon earth destroyed some, inflamed others, and cleansed still more, but with the coming of His own Son, a fire would be cast on earth that was to bring about a universal conflagration, separating mankind in two. God's Presence has that effect. Like fire it is an excruciatingly painful experience for God to come close to those who have freely chosen to bar His entrance. It is hell, in fact. And for those who have known and persisted in their search for Him in the tundra of His seeming absence, the first hints of the warmth of His love come in time are exhilarating.

Those who had gathered in the Upper Room to pray and await what Jesus had promised to send them, already had the first sparks of eternal life struck in them by the Spirit, since they believed that Jesus was the Christ, the Anointed One Israel had awaited. The Spirit Gift now turned their hesitant sparks into a fire as inextinguishable as God's own eternity. And the fire could not be contained. The flames that appeared as tongues above their heads

made each of them epiphanies of the Fire of Love that
is the Presence of God in men. What was simply a spark
is now a flame and would become a conflagration. His
followers could now see that they were to be the bearers
of the fire that he was to cast on the earth. The theophanies of God, henceforth, were to be people in whom His
presence had come to dwell. They cannot confine within
themselves, or keep under wraps, the fire within. They
are now like lamps placed on lampstands where all could
see them and be illumined by their Gift. They would
pierce the powers of darkness that enveloped the earth
as a shroud envelops dead men's bones.

A fire not only illumines, it also consumes. The tongues
of fire might also be seen as consuming the dross of false
self-conceptions that are produced by one's own egotism
and an unbelieving heart. All of the securities not rooted
in God but in the self are drawn toward the fire of the
Spirit, tested, and either consumed or purified. These
include all of one's most treasured loves, the Isaacs that
we judge to hold the promise of the future.

"THEY WERE ALL FILLED WITH THE HOLY SPIRIT" (v. 4).

The import of the event of Pentecost is that life comes
to the inert, power to the impotent, enthusiasm to the
bewildered, boldness to the timid, and huddled men go
forth to proclaim the deeds done in their midst. The
change in the disciples of Jesus is remarkable. They are
transformed from being loyal but ineffectual followers
into sent and driven men. If there had been no Pentecost,

they would still have had much to tell men about Jesus, since they were so well informed about him. Aside from their fresh memories of what he had done as well as what he had told them, they would have been able to assure the universe that he had risen from the dead, since they experienced him after his death. But there is a world of difference between being informed and being inspired. Before Pentecost, they had knowledge about Jesus and they had faith in him and love for him. But now Love has them, trust will undergird their lives, and Truth will impel them to speak out and teach them what to say. They are now in on the conspiracy between Jesus and the Spirit, and Jesus and his Father, because the Spirit has been sent into their hearts.

Unlike the mysteries in the life of Jesus of Nazareth, all of which are unrepeatable since they are inalienable mysteries of his own person, Pentecost is repeatable and is being repeated even now. The Spirit has not ceased to assume the startling immediacy with men that began that morning in Jerusalem when men staggered as if they were drunk, so forceful was the Power they were receiving.

It would be difficult to determine which of the two aspects of the mystery of Pentecost is the more remarkable: the fact that in an unprecedented way the active Power and Presence of God should have erupted so forcefully in the human order, or that the Holy Spirit should have come to men, not only come *to* men but *into* men, not only into men but operated immediately through men.

This should not cease to be a matter of stupefaction to us that the Spirit of God should be present in and course through the world by means of persons and communities. The Divine Power limits itself to the width and heighth and depth of the sails thrown up to catch the Wind. It chooses to limit itself to the limits men place upon God, in order to work with, rather than in spite of, the work of His hands. This awesome descent is a measure of the dignity of the human person in God's eyes and the humility of the Spirit, who both "obeys" the Senders and submits to the frailty of those to whom It is sent.

To be on our side of reality, the Spirit has to undergo a kind of kenosis with each indwelling, an emptying of Its wholly Holy Otherness (without, at the same time, surrendering Its Sovereignty). Its self-abasement is not unlike the emptying the Logos underwent when, willing to forego equality with God, he assumed the form of a man. In a sense the Spirit puts Itself at the mercy of our sinfulness, since each of us makes a different amount of room in himself for the indwelling of the Spirit. Each accords a different degree of welcome. The Spirit ordinarily limits Its Presence and Its Power to the depth, length, and breadth of a man's Amen.

"[THEY] BEGAN TO SPEAK FOREIGN LANGUAGES AS THE SPIRIT GAVE THEM THE GIFT OF SPEECH. NOW THERE WERE DEVOUT MEN LIVING IN JERUSALEM FROM EVERY NATION UNDER HEAVEN, AND AT THIS SOUND THEY ALL ASSEMBLED, EACH ONE BEWILDERED TO HEAR THESE

The Personality of the Holy Spirit

MEN SPEAKING HIS OWN LANGUAGE" (Acts 2: 4–6):

What is unique about the Spirit can be seen in what is different about the followers of Jesus when the Spirit invades their spirits, moving their hearts, transforming their speech. "All began to speak foreign languages as the Spirit gave them the gift of speech. . . . How does it happen that each of us hears them in his own native language?" (Acts 2:8). One of the miracles of Pentecost was the faculty of speaking in tongues that were foreign; but another equally significant miracle was the ability to hear tongues that, though foreign, were as familiar as one's own. The gift of speech was given to some, but those from every race and nation who could hear speech in their own tongues did so with no less a gift than those who spoke. Both proclaimed the marvels of God in Jesus.

The Power that the Spirit-Gift released brought a momentary end to the babel of languages that had always symbolized man's disunity, and initiated a time of perfect and effortless communication between men. What we see happening at Pentecost to men who were strangers but now can hear and speak to one another is peculiarly the work of the Spirit, since it is peculiar to the Personality of the Spirit to knit people together, to enable relationship to grow where there were only "I's" before. The babel of languages symbolizes man's incapacity to be present to another as himself and to have the other present to him as other. When presence to one another is rare or superficial, we are hearing and speaking foreign languages to each other.

Something of the measure of the failure of the Christian community to be the bearer of the Spirit in Power is the fact that foreign languages are increasing alarmingly among us. Languages that are foreign to the hearer are heard in every home and on every street, between races, classes, generations, and nations. The frequency with which men wage war is only a surface indication of the pervasive and cavernous incapacity of human beings, unaided, to speak to and be heard by one another, whereas the hunger to do so is epidemic. The need to hear the other and be heard as oneself extends to every international, interreligious, interacial, interethnic, and interpersonal level of human interchange. If love of one another is to mean anything, it must begin with this capacity.

"WE HEAR THEM PREACHING IN OUR OWN LANGUAGE ABOUT THE MARVELS OF GOD" (v. 11).

The same content was heard by many and spoken by a few: "the marvels of God." Although the event of Pentecost is the epiphany of the Spirit, it should not be a matter of surprise to us that the recipients of the Spirit-Gift immediately advert more to the marvels done in Jesus by the Father than they do about the Spirit Itself. The reason has already been pointed out. The Holy Spirit effects in others what It is in Itself. The Witness creates witnesses. It does in time what It is from all eternity. The result of the Spirit's touch is a consciousness-raising, not a consciousness of the Spirit as such, but a profound awareness of and capacity to witness to Jesus and his Father, and to love the self that is the recipient of such love.

Beady-eyed, teeth-gritting, self-loathing, man-deprecating witnesses are not the witnesses we are referring to. The witnesses that the Spirit's coming creates are lovers; they are experiencing God as Love and themselves as being loved. We witness to what we love, whether we realize it or not. We inevitably point to where our hearts are by the things we say and do. The effect of the Spirit on a man is that his loves change or get rearranged, and everything about him points to that which is changing in him and to the new comprehension of his own lovability.

Our loving and our witnessing, therefore, are intimately related. The sign of the Spirit's activity is our love for the authentic self into which God is pouring his own goodness as well as our love and praise for the only Son of the Father and the Father of this only Son. Those who either have not received the Spirit or have willfully truncated Its Power in them are illegible signs if their loving fails to witness or their witnessing fails to be loving. This is not a moral axiom or a new "ought" to be observed but a simple observation about how to detect the presence or absence of the Spirit's activity. A witnessing to God's love that does not derive from the Spirit will eventually not be credible. The massive, general reluctance of the majority of Christians even to point to, or confess God's love of them to others, suggests that they have yet to receive the Power they need to become what they already are in God's eyes and do the work of loving in His name.

c. The New Consciousness

We must break into its component parts this new consciousness, this transfiguration of the interior universe that happens in the Pentecost moment. The Spirit, first of all, illumines the Personality of God as transcendent Goodness, alias Father. "God has sent the Spirit of His Son into our hearts: the Spirit that cries: "Abba, Father" and it is this that makes you a son, you are not a slave any more; and if God has made you son, then He has made you heir" (Gal. 4:6–7).

The heightening of the consciousness of God as one's Father should produce a radical change in one's self-understanding. To give an intellectual assent to the theological datum that one is a child of God is a far cry from the experience of one's contingency and dependency on an infinitely good Father. The revolution in one's own self-understanding, in turn, produces a trial of all the other images of the self that one has entertained. "Unless a man becomes as a little child he shall not enter the Kingdom of heaven" (Mt. 18:3). Insofar as man can be one with the conspiracy of the Spirit that has been sent into his heart and say "Father", to that extent the Kingdom is his own. He then does not need to collect booty to surround himself with ego supports since, as heir, he knows there is nothing in the Kingdom that will not be his.

But we are not isolated children of the Father nor individual heirs of the Kingdom. We are sons in His son and heirs with him. The first outpouring of the Spirit is accompanied by a completion of understanding of who Jesus was and what the Father did to him in view of his obedience. Having raised Jesus from the dead and exalted him "at His own right hand," the Father bestowed upon him the name that is above every other name, because it was the Father's own name: Lord.

The ability to perceive this, to penetrate to the final identity of Jesus, was not a matter of analysis or theological acumen but Gift. "No one can say 'Jesus is Lord' unless he is under the influence of the Holy Spirit" (I Cor. 12:3). It would have been preposterous to have reasoned to such a stature for Jesus, one that had him raised above and placed over every order of being in the created universe, the Lord of all that was, or is or ever will be. What reason could not even imagine, our Spirit-enlightened faith can assert boldly.

But the ability to say that Jesus is Lord, like the ability to speak the name "Father" of God, is not merely an identification made of two Divine Persons through "the Spirit who reaches the depths of everything, even the depths of God" (I Cor. 2:10). This identification cannot be made without a corresponding gift enabling one to surrender his own life into the hands of Jesus as his Lord. The title itself presumes a surrender if the user of the title is describing the condition of his heart. One has ceased being lord of his own life and has desisted in trying to exercise sovereignty in his own regard. Accompanying the Spirit-borne understanding that Jesus is Lord is the choice freely made to lose my own footing to walk in him.

But the beautiful thing about Pentecost is that Jesus, who is now seen as Lord, is not on some far-away throne hoping for eventual arrival of his followers. He is with them now. The Sent has brought the Sender. The Promised One has brought the Risen One. God's own Spirit has kept Emmanuel, God-with-us, from being a preposterous sacrilege. He is not present as some phantom energy in a nebulous order of existence, but he is with them (as he is with us) as who he is, the Lifted-up-one who is drawing all of them and all things to himself. His presence was most palpable when they celebrated "the breaking of the bread" as he had commanded. There is no presence of the Risen Jesus to men except through the Spirit. And there can be no way of validating the claim that one has the Spirit unless this is accompanied by signs of the presence of Jesus.

The entire process of differentiation of themselves from Israel begins the moment his followers start to comprehend the implications in the title of Lord now assigned to Jesus. Although they would not have said so explicitly in the first few years (since it was still too indistinct and they were still too univocally monotheistic to articulate it), if Jesus was Lord and Yahweh was also Lord, then Jesus must be on a par with Yahweh and equally worthy of our worship and adoration.

In all of this expanded consciousness of the Divine Reality, the Spirit is not directly in our consciousness. It is pointing to the way of our salvation, while staying in the background. The lines of Isaiah describe the Spirit's inevident position to us in the ongoing mystery of Pentecost: "Whether you turn to right or left, your ears will hear these words behind you, 'This is the way, follow it'" (Is. 30:21).

Another component of the experience of Pentecost is the freedom each of the recipients feels in his own person and with his religious tradition. They show themselves free of the letter in the way they now see and use Scripture. They show themselves free to proclaim to others him whom they have followed, the one whom Israel awaited. Peter's speech is bold with accusation of those who had Jesus crucified. "You killed him" (v. 23). But it is bolder still in the claims it makes about the man from Nazareth. Instead of cowering before the inquiry of a single servant girl, Peter is now free of any fear of the authorities. He announces forthrightly for all Jerusalem to hear: "The House of Israel can be certain that God has made this Jesus whom you crucified both Lord and Christ" (Acts 2:35). They soon will show themselves free of the temple and, being themselves temples, be ready to proclaim their Lord to the four corners of the earth as the Spirit's Power gives them wings. They show themselves free to discard the old wineskins, which cannot do justice to the new wine of his abiding presence. Those who insisted on trying to catch the new wine in their well-worn categories would find that their bones remained dry and their thirst unslaked. Those who were not free were able only to judge "drunk" of those who were.

Freedom is not only a gift of the Spirit, it is what the Spirit is. It re-creates Its own traits in those who welcome

It. So, as Paul notes, "where the Spirit of the Lord is, there is freedom" (II Cor. 3:18).

This new gift of freedom is not given them with the intention that they should taunt those still under the slavery of the Law. Their freedom is a power for them to assure others that there is a fuller way of living and that the constricted categories that keep them bound in their relationships to God and one another are unnecessary shackles. "For me there are no forbidden things," Paul would later explain. But his freedom would not be an occasion for offending others still unsure of their gift. Rather, it would be an occasion for loving them. "True, there are no forbidden things, but it is not everything that helps the building to grow" (I Cor. 10:23).

Pentecost was a jail break! What had bound them was now loosened. Their dancing feet, marveling tongues and exuberant hearts were the evidence that bound men were now free. Free from what? From the images that they had entertained about themselves.

Or, to change the metaphor, Pentecost was the moment in which the new Breath which was breathed into them drove out all the poisonous fumes of negative self-images they had unwittingly inhaled from their milieu and each other. There is considerable evidence in the Gospels of the apostles' attitudes toward themselves. Their anxiety, for example, about who was to be the greatest in the Kingdom that was being established was not naked ambition but the need to cover over personal disesteem by position. Henceforth, the beatitude will be: Blessed is the man who is poor in or free from the inhalations of false attitudes toward himself. Cursed is the man, on the other hand, who is rich in lies about his own identity. The joy of the Kingdom belongs to those to whom it has been given to inhale the truth about themselves. The limitations that are imposed by each baptized Christian on the power of the Spirit that would operate new Pentecosts in each of us come not so much from our sinfulness, I suspect, as from our unwillingness to entertain the view of ourselves that God has of us. The Spirit's power in us is meant to provide an alternative to self-definitions that are fallacious and, consequently, unfreeing.

The final component of the Pentecost event was social. The many experienced themselves as one. Individuals became one because the Spirit that was now animating them was making them one. Though they each had a particularity and a uniqueness that was irreversible, they were also in such unison that one body was an apt metaphor to describe them. They were also of one heart and mind about their collective identity, as well as single-minded about the direction they were to take. "The faithful all lived together and owned everything in common" (v. 44). Being present to the Lifted-up one as who he was, the Spirit continually led them to become who they were, his Body, his Bride, his very own flesh animated by his Spirit. It was by their being present to him through the Spirit that they were made one; they received their unity, they did not achieve it by seeking it.

By being faithful to his Risen Presence drawing them to Himself, these Pentecost Christians had their relationships to one another transformed. They became more and more closely knit, praying together, committing themselves to one another, sharing their belongings with one another, even their own food and shelter. Their new capacity for relationship with one another was one of the results of the gift his Presence brought them through the Spirit that breathed as one in them. His Presence was also summons to become and freely accept what they were being made. To the degree they would fall away from being one, to that extent his Presence among them would be diminished. Just as the Trinity is Three in One, so the community that is many in its members must be one.

The Spirit came to the community, not to individuals. Though the Risen One appeared to individuals before he sent his Spirit, ever since this moment, individuals receive the Spirit and the presence of the Risen One, only through the community. The Spirit animates a Body, not monads. Each new cell or dead cell comes to life through the touch of other members of the Body of Christ who are animated by the Spirit. Even the audacious singularity of Paul, the Apostle, had to await the ministrations of Ananias before he could be baptized and filled with the Holy Spirit. The loner who claims he is being led by the Spirit is a liar.

So much for what we can learn about the Personality of the Spirit from Its primary breakthrough into the affairs of men, the event of Pentecost. When added to the previous observations, this concludes some of the things that we can say about the Personality of the Spirit. Words about the Spirit as a Person tantalize us more than satisfy us. Ideas about the Spirit cannot contain the comprehensions they promise any more than sails can become containers of the winds they catch. We trespass if we seek to know the Spirit without the Spirit. The only valid way of inquiry is by asking the Spirit to teach us about Itself and Its ways. If It can teach us "all things" It can shed a little light, notwithstanding its transparency, on Itself and how it goes about teaching us who we are in the eyes of both our Father and our Lord as well as who They are.

IV

Contemporary Spiritualities and the Spirit

One need not be a wizard to detect that all is not well in Holy Mother Church. For a community that was to be of one mind, it has, more often than not, been a spectacle of divisiveness in recent years. If we really are Christ's Body, animated by one Spirit, how explain the many confusing, even scandalous conflicts that have erupted throughout the past, with the past decade not the least of the times to be explained.

There are, of course, as many explanations of why we have found ourselves in these straits recently as there are conflicts. "Merely a symptom of the alienation that faces every institution in society," the observer of culture suggests, not without a good deal of evidence to support his contention. "The conflict is between two ecclesiologies," others suggest, "with the people of God idea at enmity with the hierarchical ecclesiology of another age." Notwithstanding the many explanations, the most popular way of labeling the conflicts has been: "Progressives" are locked in mortal strife with the "Liberals."

Labels sometimes describe the realities they are fitted to; but at times they distort our ability to examine reality also. If the labels used to describe conflicts are inaccurate, they add to the conflict by removing our eye from the reality to be observed so that we can paste our judgments onto it.

This chapter will make the simple contention that conflicts have been traced to the wrong level of the life of the Church. The labels used, furthermore, to describe these inaccurately located disharmonies are misleading and have served to exacerbate them. When the source of the differences among us is accurately located and labeled properly, our ability to love or at least have respect for one another will be helped immeasurably. And the price of that love or respect will not require that we surrender where each of us lives and moves and has his being-with-God to achieve a false kind of harmony with one another. And, finally, we will attempt to spell out the connection between our findings and the Spirit's role.

Conflicts about doctrine, the pace of renewal, tradition, theology, the kind of authority those who hold offices in the Church should have and how it should be exercised, are all effects, it seems to me. Underneath these there is the key difference: how one images God, approaches Him, experiences Him, and articulates this experience to oneself. Conflict in the Church should be traced to the level of spirituality, in other words. By spirituality I mean primarily how one relates to God and how he views himself and others as a result of this relationship. Everyone who believes in God lives according to some spirituality in the sense that he has received or developed some understanding of the Supreme Being and relates to Him in terms of that understanding.

If the observation that our differences are as profound as the way we view and relate to God, coincides with the reader's own observations, proof will be superfluous. If it does not, I would not know how to go about proving the point. Suffice it to say here that if there were general agreement that spirituality is the source of our differences, we should then have a new reason to listen to each other despite our differences (without either denying them or trying to realign them), since the area of a person's relationship to God is relatively inviolate, we would all agree.

Now for the labels. I do not think those can be proved either, but simply stated. They will either fit comfortably into what one experiences in the people he knows and the Christian communities of which he is a part, or they will not. It seems to me that there are at least three main spiritualities that are the ordinary ways in which contemporary Christians image and relate to God and ultimately see themselves and others. These three spiritualities could be described as programmatic, autogenous, and pneumatic.

By programmatic spirituality I mean one in which the person's experience of God has come about in and through the Church. The medium in which his relationship with God has been developed and is sustained is ecclesiocentric. His responses to God, whether liturgical, devotional, moral, or doctrinal, have been framed for him by the teaching, visible Church. Obedience is the sun around which all the other virtues in his galaxy of

Christian virtues turn. Because he identifies with the Church, the emotion of loyalty rises easily in his heart. He will speak readily about the Church but with some hesitation about his experience of God, since he has come to rely on the responses given him to supply for his own words in this area.

If he is a Roman Catholic, the Gospels are generally used sparingly by him to nourish his piety, since the Church is the mediator for him. Besides, private interpretation has proven the bane of her uneven history, has it not? He welcomes renewal, but would be suspicious of anything that passes for renewal that has not been validated by, or shaped by, the official Church. The new Jerusalem that is coming down from above descends on us, as it were, through the papal steeple, the episcopal nave, and the clergy-filled sanctuary. He believes that this is the shape of the community Christ founded. This is the form that Christ willed, and he will remain faithful to it till the end of time.

As a spirituality its strengths are perseverance, docility, order, and reverence for tradition. If there were something intrinsically wrong about a programmatic spirituality, then all sacraments would be sacrilegious, all our creeds blasphemies and the objects of devotion idols. Those who disdain the programmed responses of the Church could be equivalently denying that God has been present or acting in his community in the past.

But a programmatic spirituality can also produce a negative yield. When the responses hallowed by usage and the sanction of the Church are used as excuses for not developing the person's own unique relationship with

God, or when the doctrinal, devotional, moral, liturgical, and vocational responses that the received tradition bequeathed to contemporary Christians are used as a shield to withstand the Spirit then the negative yield begins. When programmatic responses are used to substitute for and intercept new invitations of the Spirit, then righteousness has fallen back into the hands of men, and a sterile Church begins to exist for its own sake. God will then be experienced as the One Who acted, and our celebration will be of the used-to-be, not of a Divine Breath breathing new life, eternal love, and the hint of His infinite peace into us now. When in practice it becomes ideal for the received tradition to be passed on exactly as it has been received, then the Bride of Christ, the Church, becomes sclerotic, and the Spirit that is to animate her life recedes to the barely detectable inner life of the community. If things come to such a sorry state, then what poses as fidelity to Christ will flow not from love of him, but from love of the past, from the need for security rather than faith, from law rather than Spirit. Yesterday's means can easily become ends in themselves today; what had been found helpful in deepening previous generations' union with God can become ways of establishing one's credentials with men tomorrow.

The second kind of spirituality operating in today's Christian population, the one I call autogenous, is one that by definition has its origin in the self. Not the self of the flesh in Paul's sense, but the self that is open to and hungers for meaning. Since the devotee of this spirituality views the teachings and the practices of the Church selectively, it is fair to say that the locus of authority has shifted from the Church to himself. There is a difference between the faith horizon he has been taught and the one he operates on. He neither denies nor affirms the majority of things he was taught. They are simply inoperative in his life. He does live a life of faith while the "oughts" and "ought nots" that he received from the teaching Church in his younger days are being transformed, interiorized, or disregarded by him. His horizon is filled with the truths that he has personally come to believe in. He believes in them to the extent that he has been able to educe meaning from them.

The medium in which he approaches and experiences God is the making of meaning. As far as the virtues are concerned, he would probably put responsible social action ahead of the traditional ones. The institutional Church itself would be constantly judged by him according to its capacity to act meaningfully and justly on the world. Since he has achieved adulthood, he is not loath to spell out for her some of the "musts" and "must nots" the institutional Church might observe.

His relationship to God would not be accurately described as an affective one. God is the source of meaning to him and the only way of seeing the world as having any intelligibility. He scrutinizes the activity of prayer more often than he prays, since it still suffers from being among the "oughts" of his past. God affirms him and bestows a feeling of worth upon him, not a sense of sinfulness. Rather than musing for any length of time on God's transcendence or expending much energy on the praise of Him, he feels more comfortable with the idea that God is glorified by the way he uses his talents. Man's secularity and his responsibilities to his fellow man are "where it's at" for this man.

The ranks of this spirituality are swelling. Many who view God, and consequently themselves and their fellows, in this optic do so in reaction to the limitations they were being subjected to by rigid proponents of programmatic spirituality. Something of their numbers and a bit of their mentality can be read in the worldwide phenomenon in Roman Catholicism of diminished numbers of penitents. Their selectivity may also be apparent in the fact that the number of communions has not fallen off but even risen proportionately.

Autogenic Christians have been behind most of the social causes that have sensitized the Church and assisted the world in recent years. The causes of peace, civil rights, ecology, the needs of the Third World, and the innumerable causes of justice that come and go as unevenly as the injustices that provoke them into being, have all received the attention and concern that many whose spirituality is autogenic have brought to them.

Perhaps even a larger portion of the population of autogenics are those who have a particular interest in theology. These would often have a difficult time keeping their taste for theology from becoming a substitute for acts of faith, hope, and love arising from the theological powers infused in them at baptism. One of the main weaknesses of autogenic spirituality is its penchant for making what goes on in one's mind or what one does with one's feet the totality, the only thing that a life of faith is meant to be. On the other hand, a capacity for understanding the teleology of the universe and acting on it, concern for responsible action on behalf of one's brother, and enlightened stewardship over created reality are some of the strengths of this self-starting spirituality.

The third kind of spirituality operating in the Christian community might be accurately described as pneumatic, since those living its style of response to God claim to have a sense of the immediacy of the presence of Risen Lord that only the Spirit can produce. Hence the word pneumatic. They do not live according to the meaning their understanding educes from the gift of faith but according to a felt knowledge, an inner unction the Spirit provides. Affective prayer is the medium in which they experience God.

The pneumatic reveres the Church no less than the programmatic Christian, but it plays a different role in his life. Though seeing himself as a member of the Church, it does not, as an institution, impinge on his consciousness to any great extent. The teaching Church provides him with out-of-bounds markers, which he observes, but he is so taken up with the drama going on within those boundaries that he scarcely alludes to them. The markers are not a source of tension to him.

Like the autogenous Christian, the pneumatic is an inner-directed man, but the inner to which he attends by prayer is "the Beyond within." His experience of God is primarily one of Christ, not the Christ who lived but who lives now and acts in him through the Spirit. It is the experience of a yoke that is light, a companionship of unequals become as one because Love has made them so. In their relationship the initiative belongs to Christ, while expectancy and active receptivity toward him are the constant dispositions of the person.

He reveres action no less than the autogenic Christian but weighs its value on different scales. It must spring from, be carried on by, and reach its completion within the affective experience of companionship with Christ. Activity that is not animated by that experience or diminishes it is considered inadequate. Activity that weakens the bonds of affectivity is either brought within the pale of companionship or discontinued. In the course of weighing what actions his companionship with Christ is calling him to, the moral conscience has little to do, since right and wrong are not a tension the pneumatic is usually laboring under. Discovering the origins of the ideas and moods he experiences, on the other hand, is of great importance to him. A faculty of discernment develops in pneumatics, since they are concerned with the direction in which God is calling them.

"Pneumatic" should not be equated with "pentecostal," it may be noted. Many of the responses of Pentecostal Christians derive directly from the programmed responses that sectarian Pentecostalism has developed. Those whose experience of God is framed in and by these responses are living a programmatic rather than a pneumatic spirituality, no matter how Spirit-centered they claim to be. Not everyone who cries "Lord, Lord"— or "Spirit, Spirit," in other words—should be numbered in the ranks of those living a pneumatic spirituality. What is presupposed for a pneumatic spirituality is an unmediated experience of God in Christ over a sufficiently long period of time, so that the metaphor "companionship" becomes an accurate description of their interior life. Their experience of God is such that it is inexplicable by anything that could come from autosuggestion or a group-induced response.

A pneumatic spirituality, however, seldom begins in and certainly cannot be long sustained by the solitary individual. It presumes community. Two (spouses, for example) or three or more must be gathered together in His name in order for the possibility of an intimate relationship with God to be either entertained or sustained. Their ability to confirm, confront, and affirm one another in this spirituality is a *sine qua non* of its continuing. It would appear that many Christians, for fleeting moments of their lives, live a spirituality that could be accurately named pneumatic but, in sensing its difference, do not trust the experience, and revert to the surer footing of either of the other two.

The weaknesses of pneumatic spirituality are in its penchant for spiritualizing reality. It can become anti-Incarnational, be deficient in a sense of the larger ecclesial community, or be historically myopic. Its devotees can also make claims of inspiration that are relatively immeasurable by others. The strengths of the pneumatic are the primacy of love of God that it strives for, its Trinitarian emphasis, the centrality of prayer, and its capacity for building strong Christian communities.

Pneumatic communities come about as a result of a similar interiority, a common need, and the disponibility of each of the members to the Lord Who makes them one. It is not the commitment of the members to one another that creates these communities, nor does it

The Conspiracy of God

maintain one in existence after it has begun. Mutual commitment is one of the effects of being led to come together, not a cause of that coming together. This effect continues as long as there is a sense of certainty that He is leading the individual members of the community in the same direction.

a. Contrasting the Three Spiritualities

So much for a general description of each of the three main spiritualities I see operating in the Christian communities. Every Christian whose faith is operative lives according to one or other spirituality, and perhaps the majority would be accurately described by one of the above three. It should be immediately obvious that it is a case of more or less, and that living according to one does not tightly preclude some experience of the other two. It is a question of the predominant medium in which a man experiences God. Rather than playing one off against the other two, the reader will see that some of the predominant features of each are endemic to Christianity itself. The characteristics of one do not deny the value of the other two, but each has emphases that make it distinctive and potentially enriching to the other two. By contrasting them with one another this could become more evident.

In terms of time, the programmatic's reverence for the guidance of the Church tends to make him past-oriented. The autogenic's concern for responsible action makes him focus on the present. And the pneumatic's sense of

106

expectancy that God will take the initiative makes him future-oriented.

The relationship of each spirituality to the Church and its directives will be somewhat different also. Those groups whose style of spirituality is predominantly programmatic will be concerned with implementing the directives that come to them from higher-ups. The decision-making process, such as it is, of such a group will be deductive. The decision-makers will ordinarily be the clergy. The overarching decision of the programmatic group or the leaders of such a group which, in turn, is acquiesced in by the members, is one that stresses the universality of the Church. It is saying, in effect, that it sees itself as one cell in a worldwide organism. Innovation or the factor of self-determination is reduced to practically nothing in this group's style of operation. The majority of parishes in this country would seem to fit this description, at least within Roman Catholicism.

A group of Christians whose predominant spirituality is autogenous, on the other hand, will take what the hierarchical Church has to say as a starting point. It will be given as much weight as its ability to elicit meaning for them, rather than the meaning the hierarchy assigns it. Autogenous groups exemplify the ecclesiological truth that the Church is a community of communities. These groups would stretch the meaning of self-determination to the limits and see this as their way of assuring full responsibility for the Gospel and the mission of the Church.

Pneumatic groups will seek out the specifically religious value in the teachings and directives of the Church. Their enthusiasm for these will be in proportion to their ability to provide spiritual insight or motivation or unction. But in addition to the hierarchical authority of the Church, these pneumatic groups will be on the lookout for and accord authority to the gifts God gives to the individuals in their communities for the upbuilding of the Body of Christ. In this they exemplify the ecclesiological reality of the Church as built up on a multiplicity of gifts, or the Church as charismatic as well as institutional.

The style of decision-making of each Christian group is another indication of the kind of spirituality it exemplifies. Group decisions are made by pneumatics in an atmosphere of prayer, by autogenics in an atmosphere of reason, and by programmatics in an atmosphere of obedience. Communal discernment will be a favored technique of the first; discussion of the second; while the intentions and mind of the hierarchy will be the major concern of the third.

The experience of community is different in each of the three. The pneumatic community is open to being led as a group in its prayer and the direction it takes. This presumes a considerable amount of commitment to one another and unity in the Lord. There are a growing number of such communities in this country.

Programmatics are no less committed to the Lord, but they do not seem to have a need for relationships with others in which there is an explicit sharing of their faith. Nor do they experience Christian community in any tangible sense. The unity of Christians is something they believe in, not something they feel they have to strive to experience personally. The group they worship with is usually constituted by geography, that is, the parish.

They can be highly motivated with regard to the faith and be relatively passive with regard to fostering relationships with their fellow parishioners. Part of this is, of course, the anonymity that urban life or huge parish plants fosters rather than something that is properly traced to the level of spirituality.

Many groups of Christians call themselves Christian communities whose characteristics are more evidently autogenous than pneumatic. They are together to accomplish a common task, perhaps even because of a common history, such as religious orders enjoy. They may remain together because of their commitment to serve the Lord together in the tasks the group undertakes without ever having the experience of being moved *as one* in prayer or to service. If this experience of being moved *as one* were a common experience in the group, they would be a pneumatic community.

The autogenic is desirous of sharing his ideals, principles, and insights. He sees himself as responsible as anyone else for the mission of the Church. He approaches the task of planning it discursively, with an emphasis on reasoning and prudence. He leaves implicit or takes his faith and that of others for granted in drawing up what is to be done. His faith may have led him to act, but he does not see that it could impregnate the shape of the action to be undertaken, or at least not explicitly. Relationships in groups of autogenics are built primarily on task. Their communities are *ad hoc* and ordered to objectives first and foremost, and being present to one another only secondarily.

One final point should be made about people who,

though perhaps claiming otherwise, are really outside of the pale of any of these spiritualities because of something in them that vitiates a life of faith. The programmatic can harbor persons who have never transcended their conditioning either because they lacked the educational opportunities that would have made such transcendence possible or because they chose the security that total conformity to the programmatic afforded. The autogenous category can harbor those who are not motivated in any way by faith that is the gift of God but merely by philosophical excogitations on the faith. Christianity could be merely one of the several meaning systems these people feel at home in, and their religious selectivity could be simply philosophical eclecticism. Finally, the seeming pneumatic can be himself delusional. Persons attempting to live this kind of spirituality seem to be more susceptible to illusion and illuminism probably because their sense of the world of spirits is heightened. They can also be the most stubborn of the three in withstanding the legitimate critique of others.

b. A Common Enemy and a Common Summons

There might be some merit in grading these three spiritualities as good, less good and least good, if we were talking about abstractions. But since we are talking concretely and about where people are, there seems to be no justification for such grading. It certainly is not within the prerogative of any of us to snub another's relationship to God nor to judge it. And it does no good for the person himself to denigrate his own conception and experience of God, or another's, for that matter.

None of the three develops independently of needs. Each is a mixture of lights and shadows, biases and experiences, personal histories and innocence of history. Their distinctiveness can flourish as much by the absence of sight as by insight. The failure to be aware of others' experience of God can also be a reason for distinctiveness proliferating.

Each of the three, though internally different, has a common enemy. That enemy is an egotism that would subjugate the Presence received to a manageable content. Faithlessness under the guise of faith, wherein God becomes an object rather than a presence, can affect all three. God's immediacy is the glory of our reality as men. It is the heart of the Good News. It is the pinnacle of human fulfillment. We are highly skilled at avoiding this immediacy of relationship that God calls all of us to and that He makes possible in His Son through His Spirit. Part of our adroitness in avoiding this immediacy is in denying that we are prone to do so or guilty of having done so. Every cunning, every stealth of our unregenerate self is marshaled against the immediacy of relationship with the Other as Other, since we are constantly seeking to substitute our image for the reality. Rather than being present with their hearts, many will use their memory as a substitute for the experience of immediacy. Many too will use their imaginations to conjure up a presence of their own making which, though unreal, is more easily managed. But neither of these powers of man works. It is only by the power of the Spirit that a man is able to stand in and bear the immediacy of God's presence. This Artist of intersubjectivity hallows out a place for the Other as Other by indwelling the person, being on *this* side of the relationship between God and man without ceasing to be God. Man would be annihilated by God's Presence if the Spirit did not create a capacity for the Uncreated in us.

Without the Spirit, substitutes for God's Presence proliferate. Since we will not let Him be present as Who He is, we try to render Him present as who we make Him. We force the Infinite into finite forms, foolishly thinking He goes along with this ruse. Take, for example, the title "Lord," and how it can be subjected to our faithless finitizing process. It can be used today to express and accurately describe my complete and unqualified acceptance of the presence of God in Christ as Lord of my life. Tomorrow it can become an empty name, piously used but without expressing the kind of relation that the title connotes.

It is scary to say "Yes" to being possessed. It is easier to possess. It is beautiful to receive the Presence of the Other but difficult to let Him remain Other. It is the Spirit that enables us to say: "Be it done unto me according to your word," and then continues on allowing that word to be itself as it continually grows in us.

Man is essentially a becomer; it is natural for him to be ever in the state of winding down and falling away from the fading present and turning toward and entering into the inbreaking now. If he resists becoming, he will miss the meaning of being alive. If he accepts it, he must accept all the leavings it entails and the enterings it involves. The man who resists becoming closes his hands on the Other (who will not be possessed) and will have to rest content with "having" an object of faith. The man who accepts becoming, lives in risk and in need. His need is for the Spirit who actualizes our becoming and gifts our risking with the Presence of the Other. If the Other were not Himself dynamic Being (Becomer), the Spirit would not have to indwell our beings, since the Other would be statically present. But He is dynamic, so It must indwell. The Spirit is the Artist of the process of becoming that our human condition is heir to. Its "groaning within us" is always the beginning of a new song in us whose melody and words begin indistinctly. Each time we fully turn in the direction It opens out to us and yield to Its melody, a new song rises full-throated from our hearts. And tomorrow we will have to leave it go, howsoever pleasing its notes have become, in order to hear again and sing still another song to the glory of God.

We have now seen the temptation that is common to the three spiritualities. There is also a common summons that comes to each of their adherents: Leave the things of God for God. Release your need to possess the Other that you might be possessed by Him. Let the object of faith become a Presence again. This release is at the heart of the repentance to which we are called each day. It is the Spirit that opens out our becoming to His inbreaking, and covers our risking with fortitude and convinces us that our open-handedness will not leave us empty-handed.

c. Further Considerations

What has all this to do with the three spiritualities? Each of the spiritualities can be a vehicle for the Presence of God insofar as its adherents are open to the Spirit who will teach them all things. There are tensions in all three, it should be noted, pulling their adherents in opposite directions. The Spirit is pulling in one direction, toward immediacy and our receiving the Other as Other, while our faithlessness is pulling against this immediacy, trying to reduce the Other to forms and formulations and the manageable. Within pneumatic spirituality, the pull can be toward escaping from the Presence of the Other as Who He is, by hiding behind claims of "having the Spirit." And there is a dynamism in the programmatic that leads it to reduce acts of faith that once expressed and completed the relationship to ends in themselves, repeated as substitutes for the meeting. There is also something Janus-like about the autogenic, since he can accept the Presence of Truth for Itself or reduce its meaning to usables. He can act in response to God's call and men's needs, or he can use action to shield himself from the Presence of the One Who acts.

None of the three spiritualities is a nest, therefore. They are each subject to tensions, and their adherents are pulled one way or the other. If God were not a living God, it would be otherwise, and the spiritualities could be nests for men to settle into. But He is a living God, and so they cannot be so used.

We have already noted some of the advantages there are in tracing our differences to our distinctive spiritualities. There are innumerable disadvantages in not doing this, disadvantages for the individual and for the Church at large.

The general Christian population's unawareness of or inattentiveness to the several valid spiritualities operating among them can be a distinct disservice to an individual who is at odds (either because of inclination or the attraction of grace) with the style of spirituality practiced by the only group and style he is familiar with. Not being able to see that there are alternatives to the only one he knows, he will frequently interpret his difference as a loss of faith or a lack of it. The absence of a felt kinship in one group, however, does not mean that his faith could not flourish if he had the support and encouragement of another group that has a different style of relationship to God.

There are also many disadvantages to the Church as a whole. Since the bulk of believers is inclined to and familiar with the programmatic style only, many people are uncomfortable with and prone to marginalize the adherents of the other two. This leaves the Church as a whole impoverished and considerably less effective, since the emphases of each of the three are necessary reminders to the other two of aspects they can be neglecting. The need to be incarnations of Christ's love for the poor and the needy, for example, is often neglected by the business-as-usual programmatic congregation. And many of the charismatic gifts of the Spirit that pneumatics are familiar with can be unsuspected by the other two.

By neglecting to appreciate the valid variation at the level of spirituality, the hierarchical Church has tended to exercise its authority in a way that is consonant with and apropos for the programmatics only. Though there is no dearth of invitation in official statements to the affectivity the pneumatic prizes and the action the autogenic seeks, their tone often has a way of presuming programmatics only are Christian, thereby jeopardizing the other two. And the manner in which Church authority tends to be exercised, and the directives of the Church implemented can be quite limiting, and debilitating for autogenics especially and pneumatics to a lesser degree.

By unwittingly constricting the area of spirituality, some of the directions the bishops themselves have proposed in Vatican II have had difficulty being implemented. Coresponsibility, to cite one example, has been jeopardized by a general bias for the programmatic. In its analogous forms in parishes, dioceses, and regions, in forums and councils of sisters, priests, and laity, coresponsibility has had difficulty being implemented because those who would assume it are frequently only programmatics with their history of ecclesial passivity. Lack of preparation for any kind of real ecclesial decision-making, when coupled with an unwillingness on the part of many of the hierarchy that the laity actually assume responsibility, has had the effect of lessening the clout that the Council and renewal could have had. Generally speaking, these forums for the implementation of coresponsibility require the contributions of autogenics and pneumatics in order to be effective, but they often find themselves operating without the help of the representatives of these two spiritualities. When the matters handled by these forums are banal, which they appear to be for the most part, the participants have a hard time staving off apathy, a mood that has been growing about this Vatican II ideal. The unenthusiastic or ineffectual response of the majority of Roman Catholics to many of the other *desiderata* articulated by Vatican II—ecumenism and dialogue with non-Christians, to mention but two—is some indication of how inveterate a passivity programmatic spirituality breeds in good Christians.

We began this chapter with the contention that the conflict in the Church must be traced to the level of spirituality. We have, as a people, tended to look everywhere else in an attempt to locate, confront, and resolve our differences. Why? Perhaps because we prefer to keep our relationship to and experience of God to ourselves. The previously noted reluctance of Christians to witness to Christ "in the world" is followed up by a general silence among Christians themselves about their relationship to God in Christ. Would it be inaccurate to suggest that this religious privatism, whether "to the nations" or among Christians themselves, has the same cause? The conspiracy of the Spirit is entered into so shallowly by the majority of Christians! If the effect of the conspiring Spirit's activity is to create pointers to God's Presence to us in Christ and witnesses who share with others what their hearts have come to know, then to the extent that the Spirit is bound in them or absent, there will be a general silence about Him, even among one's own Christian brothers and sisters.

Who Is Duped, Who Spirit-Led?

The Christian Community tends to be somewhat suspicious of Spirit talk. Any suggestion that we should accord a new degree of attention to the Holy Spirit in our lives usually evokes misgivings in the hearer. If he could articulate them they might run something like this: Who needs the excesses of enthusiasm, the pseudomysticism and illusion that have usually accompanied any enhancement of the role of the Holy Spirit in the lives of Christians? Those with some smattering of Church history could argue that the many previous versions of the inner light, the truer vision, the purer kingdom, all of which have claimed the Holy Spirit as the source of their inspiration, have done nothing but confuse and divide the Church.

But one must always resist the temptation to play God by trying to decide in advance what would be harmful for men. Rather he must be concerned to perceive what God is actually doing, difficult as that is to do, in men's lives. Many claim to see a "new age of the Spirit" dawning in our midst. For those who do not, one could argue, on the basis of the needs of the contemporary Church and culture, that it would be good if a new age of the Spirit did dawn on us, since so many of the functions theologically associated with the Spirit seem to be required more urgently than ever to meet those needs.

To an unparalleled degree, confusion and division characterize the situation of the Church of the late sixties and early seventies. Contradictory things are said in the name of Christ on almost every issue. Does this make a new age of the Spirit of Truth less desirable or even more necessary? The present confusion and division, which no one attributes to the Holy Spirit, points to the need to be more discriminating about the many voices that claim to be on the side of God and Gospel. But the gifts necessary for the development of such discrimination—counsel, knowledge, understanding, wisdom—are gifts of the Holy Spirit.

One of the marks of the maturation process in children is their growing ability to differentiate between the stimuli to which they are subjected internally and externally. So also in the life of the Christian. The capacity to discriminate between the conflicting stimuli being experienced and respond accordingly, differentiating the bogus from the authentic, is the difference between infancy and maturity in the life of faith. The capacity to hear the voice of the Good Shepherd whenever, wherever, and through whomsoever he speaks and to distinguish it from the voice of the thief is the power of discernment the Spirit gives to those who would hear the Shepherd's voice. "The one who enters through the gate is the shepherd . . . the sheep hear his voice; one by one he calls his own sheep and leads them out . . . they follow him because they know his voice" (Jn. 10:2–4).

This is not a new ability, of course, since his own have always been able to detect his voice. What is new, however, is the number of voices claiming to speak his mind. Also new is the number of those learning to distinguish between the language used and the source of its inspiration. The most devout language can cover over faithlessness or ecclesiastical manipulation. So also, the most mundane of authors can express profound evangelical understanding and the most pious frequently mouth superficial nonsense. A large portion of the flock was at one time content to follow from afar, satisfied with following other sheeps' following of him. Those who are mediators by office and those who would be mediators by reason of their theological training—both of these populations are listened to much more selectively and circumspectly today. What they attempt to teach is listened to with more refined spiritual senses or more critical intelligences and oftentimes discarded.

Any student of culture will agree that one of the unique characteristics of our age is the degree of secularity that encompasses our lives. Vatican II accepted this condition by and large, and proceeded to spell out the implications of it by plunging the community of Catholic believers much more deeply into the world of men and things. The Council Fathers began the process of dismantling the fortress that had successfully encased and preserved the faith-understanding in recent centuries. In so doing, they were following a number of the faithful who had already begun to abandon the fortress, and anticipated and endorsed what countless others would do.

Without the safeguards that a cultural Catholicism had supplied, and *mutatis mutandis* a cultural Protestantism, many found themselves in a religiously precarious situation. Those who had relied on the culture to carry them were the most alarmed. When one finds no support or power round about him, he is forced to try to find it within himself. Institutionalized values that are not interiorized are being left behind in yesterday's fortress. But the task of interiorizing Christian values has been and always will belong to the Holy Spirit. Since the moment of the Incarnation itself, what comes to be in persons that is of God is Spirit-borne.

Inside the fortress, authority's function was central. Once outside and on foot, as it were, what authority had done for us must be done more and more by us. Rather than an occasion for hand-wringing and lamentation, the new situation should be welcomed. What we are beholding is a God-initiated process of interiorization, not the end of religion nor deterioration of order, tradition, or the authority of the Church. In the ultimate unfolding of God's design the person himself is meant to be responsible for and the locus of the Spirit's own holiness, understanding, and discernment. Centuries ago the Book of Jeremiah said as much when Yahweh described the eventual religious condition of men in these terms: "Deep within them I will plant my Law, writing it on their hearts. Then I will be their God and they shall be my people. There will be no further need for neighbor to try to teach neighbor or brother to say to brother,

'Learn to know Yahweh!' No, they will all know me, the least no less than the greatest" (Jer. 31:33–34). Or in the Book of Ezekiel, Yahweh promised a relationship of God to men in which: "I shall cleanse you of all your defilement and all your idols. I shall give you a new heart and put a new spirit within you. . . . I shall put my spirit within you . . ." (Ezk. 36:25–27).

Even if one gives all the above-mentioned, disconcerting phenomena a benign interpretation and sees God actively shaping us through them in the Spirit, still one would not have any assurance that in particular instances —and they are the only ones, after all, that ever concern us—God is really behind or initiating the new situation. How, therefore, can one tell what is God-initiated in a given situation, or simply endured by Him and the product of our own delusion, selfishness, or subjectivity? Even closer to the mark, how do I know when I am being led by the Spirit? And are there signs indicating when some "spirit" adverse to the Holy Spirit is inspiring me?

a. The Origins of Our Inspirations

More than at any time in the past, it is incumbent upon individuals and the Christian community at large to concentrate on developing for itself the art of discernment. "It is not every spirit, my dear people, that you can trust; test them, to see if they come from God" (1 Jn. 4:1). We are enjoined to "test every spirit," and commanded by the Lord himself to develop a wiliness equal to the serpent's and a hypersensitivity to wolves posing as sheep.

Who Is Duped? Who Spirit-Led?

From his own experience, Jesus knew that the principle of evil entwines itself about the length and breadth of the created universe, having a particular interest in men who are opened out to the inbreaking beneficence of God. He also knew that this evil principle's ability to deceive men by camouflaging its heinousness, by always posing as an "angel of light" (or the principalities and powers of this dark world, as Paul refers to them), is greater than our own unaided capacity to perceive it.

To make the components of discernment clear, we will imagine the case of a person who is being "inspired" to an action or a devotion or a project or a vocation, but who is uncertain of the source of the inspiration. We are assuming, of course, that what he is being inspired to do or be is something good in itself. The process of discernment is not called for if that which the person is being "inspired" to do is clearly immoral, nor is it called for if he has been remiss in gathering all the necessary data for the choice that is being contemplated. The problem he poses about the source of his inspiration assumes that God leads each of us in a particular way. Likewise that Spirit helps us to become sensitive to and adept at detecting His call and responsive to His unique way with each of us. This assumption is well founded, since the deepest part of our Judeo-Christian tradition sees God's relationship to us as one of a Divine Potter shaping each of us according to His special will for us. His gentle touches of the clay of our minds and hearts indicate the shape He would have us freely become. Hence, the importance of our knowing when the touch we feel is His or from some other source.

123

There would seem to be five general criteria for detecting His touch. There are, in other words, some general ways of testing the origins of our inspiration. All of these criteria are at least implicitly understood by the majority of Christians. By being made more explicit and applied to the question of being led by the Spirit, these criteria should become more operative and deepen the ability to discern the conflicting motions of soul that go on in everyone.

The first such criterion: The Spirit of God acts in us according to the way the Spirit is in Himself. "*Agere divinum sequitur esse divinum*," if one is given to captious latinities. Although the personality of the Spirit, as we have seen, is not directly accessible to us, we know from revelation that the Third Person of the Blessed Trinity is the Spirit of Truth and Love. When the Spirit acts in the human order, therefore, It will act accordingly —speaking the truth, coming in love and leading to love and understanding both of God and self and others. The presence or absence of such qualities will suggest that the Spirit is or is not the author of the promptings being experienced.

But we know something even more specific about the Spirit, that It is the Spirit of Christ. Its concern, therefore, is to relate us ever more intimately to the person of Christ Jesus. Whatever makes us more aware of and sensitive to the Bridegroom will be the concern and the direction of the Spirit's activity. By deepening our prayer, in fact, by "praying within us," an affective connaturality develops in us whereby our hearts know his voice through the Spirit. "It feels right in the Lord," is a favorite expression of mature discerners. For the most part, discernment is not a conscious stage but is absorbed in and is an implicit part of the whole process of companionship, and love that the Bridegroom invites and, with the Spirit, effects.

At other times, his voice is less audible or not clearly his, and we need a more reflective process. It belongs to the same Spirit to develop this more deliberate process, which heightens our detection capacity and refines our spiritual senses. Suffice it to say here that the Spirit does this in ways as diverse as the number of sheep who would hear the voice of the Shepherd, calling each by name. Their ways of knowing are largely unanalyzed by them and for the most part incommunicable to others, but with his leading of them and the calling of their names can come the certainty about its source.

If the Church were without history and a series of isolated ant hills or solitary cells, we could let it go at that with each person developing his own sense of God's way of speaking to him. But the Church is the Body of Christ, animated by the one Spirit. As such it needs more objectivity than this first criterion can furnish by itself. The claim of the individual must be somehow certified by the community. And the experience of the especially gifted must be made more accessible to others so that those whose ability to detect the voice of the Lord is slight can be helped by those who have been able to spell out the process of discernment for themselves and for others. So we must go beyond this criterion.

The second criterion is closely related to the first. It began to be articulated from the first days of the Church, especially by St. Paul and the author of the first Epistle of John. According to this criterion, one tests the presumed promptings of the Spirit by looking at the effects on the person. One must first, however, look at the overall quality of the person's life. To a person in whom the presence of God is abiding, the Spirit's new promptings will come as gently and delicately as drops of water penetrating a sponge. But to a person who has willfully chosen to live a life under the sway of "the world, the flesh and the devil," the Spirit's promptings will come from without, stinging the person with remorse and a feeling of shame and confusion. The Spirit acts, therefore, according to the spiritual condition of the person being acted upon, comforting in one case and confronting in the other.

If one is abiding in God, then the person's life will manifest signs of that presence, chief among which are joy, the praise of God, and charity toward one's brothers and sisters. In the tradition of discernment, such as it is, that has developed in the Church over the course of its history, there has always been a special emphasis on the presence of joy as the inevitable accompaniment of the motions of soul that have their origin in the Holy Spirit. Not unreasonably! One need only look, for example, at the first two chapters of St. Luke's gospel. Here one sees alternately Zachary, Elizabeth, Mary, Simeon, and John, who is still in his mother's womb, all described as filled with joy as a result of the presence of the Holy Spirit in their midst.

A second effect of the motions of soul that the Holy Spirit prompts is whether they lead to praise of Christ

Jesus. "No one can say 'Jesus is Lord' unless he is under the influence of the Holy Spirit" (I Cor. 12:3). One of the reasons why the Spirit was sent into our hearts was that we might glorify Jesus. When and where there is praise of him, the presence of the Spirit is virtually assured. When an undertaking leads to glorifying him, the presence of the Spirit is likewise virtually certain. When an undertaking is begun in the name of Jesus but soon becomes identified by me as "mine," the "promptings" that are having it continue, perhaps even those that had it begin, are suspect. If the action or vocation or project is undertaken as a confession of his Lordship and continues to have such a quality about it, the chances are good that the Spirit has prompted it. By the fruit that it is producing, it is being confirmed. "So if anyone declares himself for me in the presence of men, I will declare myself for him in the presence of my Father in heaven. But the one who disowns me . . . I will disown" (Mt. 10: 32–33).

The third main effect of the Spirit's activity in the hearts of men, and one that is even more detectable than the previously mentioned fruits, is the charity or love that is shown to the brethren. The first Epistle of John states this in many different ways. "Anyone who claims to be in the light but hates his brother is still in the dark. But anyone who loves his brother is living in the light" (1 Jn. 2:9–10). This love for one another shows itself in innumerable ways. The classical locus for the many ways of brotherly love is, of course, I Cor. 13:4–7. Here Paul spells out what real love involves; it is patient and kind, never jealous, boastful or conceited; it is never rude or selfish, nor does it take offense. "Love does not take pleasure in other people's sins but delights in the truth; it is always ready to excuse, to trust, to hope, and to endure whatever comes." True brotherly love never comes to an end.

There are clear limitations, too, to the discernment of the will of God by the three main effects that have been mentioned. These are infallible signs for the over-all direction of the heart and soul of the person trying to determine God's will for him. But over-all indication of the direction that one is going in is not of itself sufficient to elucidate the specific choice or the next step one must take. Nor will it infallibly uncover the source of the conflicting promptings one is feeling at any given moment.

In addition to the two criteria (the Spirit-acts-as-the-Spirit-is and the effects on the individual), there is a third criterion for judging the activity of the Spirit. There will be a harmony between the one claiming to be moved by God and the wider range of the Spirit's activity in others, which is, of course, the growth of the Kingdom. We can be sure that the Kingdom of God will not be divided against itself. Consequently, we can be sure there will be an over-all cohesiveness in what the Spirit is prompting individuals to do and become and what their communities are about.

Since the Kingdom is not susceptible of measurement and at the same time is spoken of in such a facile way, a more proximate and tangible way of expressing this criterion is that the Spirit will prompt only what is for the upbuilding of the community. What builds the community is of the Spirit; what tears it apart cannot be. Consequently, one's willingness to listen to the believing community and test one's spirit with its wise men and those authorities responsible for the community's order and orthodoxy is a *sine qua non* for one who would live in the Spirit.

This criterion is helpful as far as it goes, but it, too, has its limitations. The upbuilding of and being in harmony with the community can mean different things to different members of the community. The two things we can be sure it always means will be: whatever leads to a greater love of the Father through faith in Jesus and whatever increases our love of one another. Harmony may be the eventual fruit, but division could be the more proximate effect. "I have not come to bring peace but the sword." We can, in the name of order and harmony, be lulled into accepting a measurement of harmony that is not born of the Spirit. The prophets, many of the saints, and Christ himself were rejected by the community of believers on the grounds that they failed to fit the prescribed measures for what constituted harmony and the upbuilding of the community. On the other hand, one who enters into conflict with the community cannot expect nor should he expect that his own claim to be following the Spirit will be given equal weight with the whole faith community's reception of the Spirit. The burden of proof that one is truly bearer of the Spirit clearly rests on the individual in such a case. His patience and acceptance of the time required for his vindication could be something of an indication to the community of the fruits of the Spirit in him. His willingness to have his own understanding tested by the community and abide for the time being with a judgment that is contrary to his own, should give the community pause and maybe even a reason to re-examine the contentions of the individual. The one who stands against the many may be a great gift to the community, a fool for Christ or just foolish. The sword can divide today so that there will be a Gospel-single-mindedness tomorrow. The fruits in the individual, the quality of his life over a long period of time, and the relationship he maintains with the community can be most helpful indices for suggesting which of these he is.

So much for the sentiments and virtues incumbent upon the individual. The community also has a responsibility vis-à-vis the individual in this discernment process. We cannot assume that such a process is being employed if the community is merely operating in a business-as-usual way, politely making marginal those members who insist on a difference that is uncomfortable for the community, whether in what he is or does or understands. The individual is not loved or reverenced if he is not heard. He is not heard if his understanding of his person or his work is merely measured for its ability to fit or not fit the status quo or the community's over-all operation. The process of hearing, tasting the good that the individual sees or thinks he sees, and confirming or denying its validity is the way the community is built up or avoids destruction either of itself or the individuals within it. The Spirit comes to the individual in love, and only the community's love will be able to detect Its activity. Anything short of love will not be an effective means for perceiving that which God has authored.

b. Two Additional Criteria

A fourth criterion for discerning the motions of the Spirit in ourselves and others is the Gospel itself. We are following Jesus, not into trackless wastes or impenetrable jungles; he has gone before us, and is going before us. A swath has been cut by him through the dense maze of human complexity. Each of the events in the life of Jesus, as portrayed in the Gospels, are meant to illumine the stretches that open out before us. It is the Spirit that turns the words of the evangelists into light. The light the Spirit brings to our understanding of the way of the Master also points up our attempts to take shortcuts or detours that lead us away from him.

The same point could be made by employing a different metaphor. Jesus is the masterpiece of the work of the Spirit. All activity of the Spirit subsequent to Jesus' ascension into glory has been a taking of the raw material of human lives and hearts that have yielded to him and fashioning in them what has been done in Jesus. While this is being done to us, we can check the progress in us and others against the masterpiece, the life of Jesus. A favorite instrument of the Spirit in fashioning us into the likeness of Jesus is the Word of God.

This most helpful criterion also has its limits. In the name of the pure Gospel, an endless number of supposed paths have been cut by the well-meaning as well as by those who have let themselves succumb to delusion. Also debilitating for the use of the Gospel as a criterion is the number of theories from fundamentalism to secularistic humanism that abound, each explaining how and whether the words of the Gospel contain and convey the revelation of the Good News. These do not constitute insuperable obstacles, of course, but they do jeopardize some of the effectiveness a less controverted use of the Gospel could have.

A fifth criterion is the nature of the salvation itself that has been won for us in Christ and that all movements of the Spirit reinforce or consolidate. We can be certain that God does not loathe the creation He has made, nor does He will the diminishment of that creation or reject the work of His hands, the apex of which is man. His will is to bring man to the wholeness that is only seed in the beginning. Jesus exhibited the wholeness that is the Father's will for His children by the way he acted on behalf of men in his saving acts. He cursed the fig tree because it did not produce figs, and he repudiated the man with the one talent for burying it. Where there was paralysis he released it, where there was withering of limbs he restored them; blindness became seeing; hunger was fed with bread; life returned where it had been lost. All of which is to say that every motion of the Spirit of Christ will be known by the fact that, like Jesus' own acts, it will bring wholeness to the human order, not diminishment. What is born from above will be perfectly contoured by that which has grown up from below. The promptings of the Spirit will not circumvent, disparage, or pervert the "nature" receiving them. Putative calls from God that diminish the hearer are not from God. Those who have to disparage the work of creation to proclaim the Kingdom miss the unity of the Divine Plan, the harmony between nature and grace, the wholeness that all Spirit activity envisions and, as such, are deluded or misinformed.

As with the other criteria, this one is good as far as it goes. Its limitation derives from the narrow way in which we too often perceive the wholeness of our beings. More often than not, ironically, it is the images we entertain about what constitutes our wholeness that militate against our achieving, or more accurately, yielding to the wholeness of the Spirit's own making. Our preconceived notions make us poor listeners to the Spirit's promptings. A paschal step, a dying, stands between the incomplete reality of a man and the glorious wholeness that God intends for him. The price is a radical openness to the reality beckoning him and a discarding of the a-priori notions that fear that God's touch diminishes man rather than completes the work of His hands.

c. A Master's Direction

But more than these general criteria are necessary in particular instances in which God's will remains unclear. A few rare individuals in the history of the Church have been able to make explicit the process of discernment forged from their own experience. Many have found St. Ignatius Loyola invaluable in this respect. He has been able to sort out and therefore help others sort out the confusing components that go into determining and choosing God's will in a given matter. Much of the follow-

ing owes its inspiration to St. Ignatius, especially to his
Rules for Discernment of Spirits that are contained in
The Spiritual Exercises of St. Ignatius (Chicago: Loyola
University Press, 1952). These rules did not derive from
theology, nor were they deduced from Church directives. They were forged from the personal, lifelong experiences that Ignatius had from the time he was a
carnally minded young romantic to the later years when
he reached the heights of mysticism.

In order to introduce the reader to the art of discernment to which Ignatius attained, we will imagine him
directing four different people, assisting them in their
attempts to make wise decisions about what God is calling
each of them to.

The spiritual condition of the first person seeking the
direction of Ignatius is neither hot nor cold but tepid. He
has not made any progress in the spiritual life, nor does
he have any great zest for a life of sin. The experience of
the sweetness of God's presence is foreign language to
him, and devil talk would smack of medievalism. His
relationship to God is largely impersonal (or pre-
personal, which might be a more apt description), a
tension between "oughts" and "ought nots." At best,
following Christ or being led by the Spirit means obeying
the authorities of the Church. He is content with following the intermediaries, other sheep in whom he places
his confidence and puts his faith. He uses "the faith" to
justify his spiritual superficiality. Ignatius would know
that God was not yet calling such a person to follow a
particular vocation since he still had not taken seriously
nor committed himself to the task of following the

generic vocation to which all Christians are called. Having failed so far to be faithful over a few things, God will not place him over any vital functions in the Body of Christ. Ignatius would have such a person first reflect on why he came into existence. He would try to have him come to see the disorder of his life and have the purpose for which he was created become a vital and operative principle for his self-understanding. He would try to have him become conscious of the Divine Persons behind the "oughts" he is in tension with so that sorrow for his sins can replace guilt.

With such a person, Ignatius would be anxious that he focus his attention for a time on the forces of evil operating imperceptibly in his life. He would suggest ways for this person to become aware of the personification of evil in the personal "kingdom of Satan," knowing that it is to Satan's advantage to remain remote, even seemingly non-existent when a person is in such a condition. From his inevident lair, Satan operates on the senses and imagination of the spiritually lethargic, proposing gratifications that keep the senses dominant and the spiritual sensibilities dulled or virtually inoperative. He knows that a disordered life is one in which the senses rule the spirit of a man. Things are chosen for their immediate delectability, so that only the physical life seems real. The here and now appears to be the only kingdom there is, and the life of the Spirit seems too remote to be of any great interest or import. An important accomplishment of "the enemy of our souls," as Ignatius refers to Satan, is to have those who live in a spiritual limbo proceed from non-experience of the Spirit and Satan to predicate a non-existence, at least in practice, of both of these ultimate principles of activity.

As Satan tries to operate surreptitiously on such a person, the Spirit operates openly usually by confronting him, stinging his conscience, giving him an appreciation of the degree of disorder of his life, accompanied by a feeling of sorrow for the distance he has allowed to develop between himself and God. In brief, the first client Ignatius deals with comes to see the personal forces vying with one another for him behind the immediate things that have circumscribed and trivialized his life.

The spiritual condition of the second man who confides in Ignatius is such that he lives a life of familiarity with God. He has learned to be open to Him, making his choices on the basis of His known will, especially as this manifests itself in the guidance of the Church in concert with the light his own conscience gives him. This second person comes to Ignatius and describes a totally unexpected experience, one that came "out of the blue," unaffected by any process of reasoning, choosing, or hoping that he had done prior to a sudden and unmistakable influx of heavenly light and joy accompanied by a certainty about a new course of action God was calling him to undertake. It is as if a seduction had taken place in which the receptive heart of the person was suddenly ravished with love and certainty that God was present and indicating His will for him.

Ignatius' judgment in this case would be that since "God alone can give consolation to the soul without any previous cause," this must be from the Holy Spirit. The Spirit is free to enter and leave and draw up into a

transcendent state of love of God one who has been made
a temple of God by God's own choice and the individual's
conscious yielding.

He would, therefore, authenticate the experience described. The only caution he would register in such a
case would be directed to the period immediately following the unmistakable experience of God's presence.
When the consolation has diminished, the person often
forms various resolutions and constructs plans that are
not necessarily intrinsic components of that which God
attracted him to initially. These subsequent determinations "may come from our own reasoning on the relations
of our concepts and on the consequences of our judgments or they may come from the good and evil spirit.
Hence, they must be carefully examined before they
are given full approval and put into execution" (ibid.,
p. 149).

It might be noted here in passing that there seems to
be an increasing number of such cases at the present time.
What is often referred to as "conversion" or more crudely
"zapped by Jesus" can be instances of these. An important
qualification, however, are the words "without any previous cause." This would rule out experiences that are cul-
turally induced or the "in thing" to do. More light will be
shed on experiences that come from within the milieu
rather than "out of the blue" by the next party to approach
Ignatius.

It should also be underscored that a greater sensitivity
to the differentiation Ignatius makes between the inbreaking moment of God's illumining action and man's out-
going response to it would do much to preserve the

individual from delusion and the Christian community from the excesses of illuminism that periodically befall it.

d. Another Client, Another Way

The third party whom we imagine seeking the counsel and gift of discernment that Ignatius possessed to a supereminent degree is in the process of a thirty-day retreat, using the *Spiritual Exercises* as his method of prayer and reflection during this time. He has undertaken this retreat to help determine what God's will for him is with respect to a state of life. No previous choice in life has been quite so total for him. And all subsequent choices will have to be in continuity with the one he is now contemplating.

The meditations he has made thus far have brought into the forefront of his consciousness the basic truths of his faith. Perhaps more than any other aspect of his faith, the retreat has made him especially conscious of the terrain of spirit that lies under the surface of his external life. He has come to see this terrain as a battle raging between the bearer of the Spirit, Jesus Christ, and one who poses as a bearer of light whose power to operate is strengthened by those who have accepted his allurements as truth.

During the period of this client's retreat, Ignatius has been looking for and instructs the retreatant to be on the lookout for what he calls consolations and desolations going on within him. The presence of these conflicting moods of soul is a manifestation to both of them that he has reached the degree of spiritual sensitivity where he can perceive that there is a struggle of conflicting spirits going on within him.

Ignatius has informed his client what he means by each of these terms: "I call it consolation when an interior movement is aroused in the soul, by which it is inflamed with love of its Creator and Lord, and as a consequence, can love no creature on the face of the earth for its own sake, but only the Creator of them all. It is likewise consolation when one sheds tears that move to the love of God. . . . Finally, I call consolation every increase of faith, hope and love, and all interior joy that invites and attracts to what is heavenly and to the salvation of one's soul by filling it with peace and quiet in its Creator and Lord" (ibid., p. 142).

Ignatius describes desolation in terms completely opposite to this. It is "darkness of soul, turmoil of spirit, inclination to what is low and earthly, restlessness rising from many disturbances and temptations which lead to lack of faith, lack of hope, lack of love. The soul is wholly slothful, tepid, sad and separated as it were from its Creator and Lord" (ibid., p. 142).

It would be misleading and erroneous to spiritualize these motions of soul to the point where they would be unlike our ordinary human emotions. Consolation is an umbrella word for a whole spectrum of positive emotions, and desolation likewise covers a broad range of negative emotions. The relationship between graces and positive emotions and temptations and negative emotions is impossible to establish in the abstract. Suffice it to say here that Ignatius is, first of all, interested in this retreatant knowing what his particular feelings are here and now. From Ignatius' experience, he believed that the locus of the Spirit's activity, as well as the evil one's, will be more evident at the level of their emotions than at the level of their pious ideas or by the presence or absence of edifying thoughts. Once the retreatant has identified his feelings, then and only then can the process of discernment, which seeks to trace the origins of these feelings, begin.

Since the spiritual condition of the man in question is one of striving to walk with Christ Jesus in the direction of his calling, Ignatius knows that the manner of the Spirit's gifts of consolation will be as gentle as a footfall fitting itself into the cadence of his walking. It would be easy enough to detect the presence of the evil spirit if he showed his colors with equal clarity. But with a person who is faithful to the relationship he is already called to and who has opened himself to a fuller presence of God, Satan's tactic is to suggest ideas perfectly attuned to the soul's mood and seemingly continuous with its faith, hope, love, and prayer. If the retreatant were dull of heart, the evil one could propose crude things to him, but, as it is, he suggests ideas and projects tinged with spiritual allure, and teeming with promise if pursued.

Ignatius cautions his client, therefore, to carefully observe the whole course of the thoughts coming into his mind and heart, from their beginning as also through the stages and turns they take. If they are insinuated into him by the evil one, they will little by little produce disquiet. When the initial sweetness wears off, he will find himself empty and desirous of not the Lord, but the sweet-ness for its own sake. If the suggested thoughts begin to produce the fruits described above as desolation, then "it is a clear sign that the thoughts are proceeding from the evil spirit, the enemy of our progress and eternal sal-vation" (ibid., p. 148), Ignatius informs him. This same enemy can also fasten onto the natural ebb and flow of our emotions, and at moments of fatigue or despondency bring the retreatant to feel repugnance for or discourage-ment about the possibility of living a life in God's pres-ence through the Spirit.

The personality and characteristics of the evil one be-gin to become clearer now. He is a coward before a show of strength and despotic in the face of timidity. He thrives in an atmosphere of secrecy, fearing detection and ex-posure. He makes adherents to the extent that he remains undetected. Consequently, we see the retreatant's need for regular communication with his director, who acts as the midwife of the choice being contemplated, primarily by bringing him to an awareness of the operations of the conflicting emotions he is feeling and, through those of the spirits possibly being experienced by the retreatant.

Why, one might wonder, if the person in question is sincerely trying to follow where God is leading him, does not God simply drench him with light and consolation so that he will know His will? It would be a simple matter if it were merely a question of determining whether one is experiencing either good feelings coming from our own dispositions or the Lord or negative feelings coming from our own history or limitations or, at times, the evil one. But it is not as simple as that. For one thing, as we have already seen, seemingly consoling feelings can come from the evil spirit. And, in addition, negative feelings can be of extraordinary value in developing a self-knowledge and breaking open the direction God is calling one to choose.

The period of desolation, therefore, is no less a time for spiritual growth than times of consolation are. Each period contains its own lessons for the following of Christ, especially if the pedigree of the influx of feelings that seem to come "from without" is correctly detected. God allows the desolation, at times, so that one can taste his dependency on God and the helplessness that is his when left merely on his own resources. The period of desolation can also be an occasion to repent for the careless use of God's gifts one might have been guilty of in the past. Times of darkness of mind and restlessness of heart can also be occasions for becoming more childlike and asking his Father in docility and humility for that which one sees he is helpless to furnish himself.

But perhaps more important than any of these, desolation can be a gift of God if the turmoil of spirit uncovers something in the person, hitherto unknown, that has been blocking his developing a relationship with God and man. The turmoil of spirit, or restlessness, may come on the occasion of his attempt to contemplate certain mysteries of the life of the Lord. In the atmosphere of the retreat, one has an opportunity to be more sensitive to the pattern of one's emotional responses. By tracing these to their roots, to the things causing a disproportionate response, one can come to greater freedom from them or at least to a realization of the tyranny they can exercise by going unnoticed. Frequently, our negative emotions are due to crabbed images of God or hatred of self or fear of accepting the limitations—the cross, if you will—that defines human existence. Whatever the many possible causes, the first step is to acknowledge the feelings, for they can be a measure of the disharmony limiting the self in relationship to God and others.

Ignatius' way of handling the experiences of consolation and desolation that are going on within his retreatant contain the core of the Ignatian wisdom for determining whether one is being led by the Spirit to this or that choice. What Ignatius, and consequently his method of discernment of spirits, assumes is that the active presence of God was or is being experienced by the retreatant. He has experienced consolation in the restricted sense that the good feelings came "from without" and, upon reflection, he can say they were from God's grace to him. There is not yet matter for discernment of spirits in the strict sense, unless this experience has been realized.

Assuming this, therefore, the relationship between the decision about which he has been deliberating and the consolation can now be seen. The retreatant is advised to project the choice being contemplated onto the horizon of consolations experienced. Although he does this merely hypothetically, he will begin to detect a harmony or disharmony between the object provisionally seen as chosen and the horizon of God's inbreaking love. If there is a disharmony between the two, it will show itself by the retreatant sensing the incongruence of the choice with God's beckoning love, or by some degree of desolation.

If these effects continue, it will indicate either that the time for the choice is not opportune in the retreat or in the person's life, or that it is the wrong choice for him to take, or that there are other options open to him that are still unexamined by him. But if the projected choice produces a sense of rightness, an increase in consolation, or simply peace, the chances of the decision being the right one for the retreatant are very good.

Karl Rahner's explanation of this moment of the retreat and the way to discern the spirits operating on the retreatant is particularly helpful. It is found in his article, "The Logic of Concrete Individual Knowledge in Ignatius Loyola" in *The Dynamic Element in the Church* (New York: Herder and Herder, 1964), p. 158: "By frequently confronting the object of Election with the fundamental consolation, the experimental test is made whether the two phenomena are in harmony, mutually cohere, whether the will to the object of Election under scrutiny leaves intact that pure openness to God in the supernatural experience of transcendence and even supports and augments it or weakens and obscures it; whether a synthesis of these two attitudes, pure receptivity to God and the will to this limited finite object of decision produces peace, tranquility, quiet, so that true gladness and spiritual joy ensue, that is, the joy of pure, free undistorted transcendence; or whether instead of smoothness, gentleness and sweetness, sharpness, tumult and disturbance arise."

The retreatant will realize that the consolation he is experiencing will not indicate to him what the object of his choice should be, but by its presence it will serve to confirm the choice being contemplated just as the absence of consolation will suspend confirmation of it. The thing he is attempting to make a decision about, therefore, is not being revealed to him by God, as was the case with the second man Ignatius dealt with. What is being weighed in this third case is whether the choice being contemplated is an appropriate and helpful means for the retreatant to take in order to pursue the end for which he was made and to which the perceived presence of God in consolation is beckoning him.

The experience of God's inbreaking love, therefore, provides the *context* for choosing rather than the *content* of the choice. There is great significance in the fact that in many, maybe most, instances, God seems more interested in supplying this context than in the specifics of the decision to be taken. One decision is as good as another, it seems, in many instances, since one means is as conducive as another for a man to attain his end. What He does have a specific will about is that all our choices be taken within the perceived context of His inbreaking love for us, through which He is calling us to Himself.

e. Discerning Discernment

There are several reasons why the Ignatian discernment of spirits does not enjoy a wider currency and prove helpful to a greater number of people. One of these, undoubtedly, is that both directors and retreatants have frequently failed to widen the meaning of consolation and desolation to include the whole range of emotionality and affectivity the person is undergoing. When this is not part of the picture, the retreatant has a tendency to "spiritualize" reality, and the director can unwittingly manipulate this unreality or misread pious sentiments as the calling of God.

Another reason for the inefficacy of the Ignatian rules may be found in the proneness of zealous men to interpret successful past formulas rigidly—in this instance, the *Spiritual Exercises*. Ignatian insight into the ways of God with men cannot be imported into the twentieth century as if we had learned nothing about the complex ways of human consciousness in the four intervening centuries. Our increased understanding about the dynamics of men's conscious and subconscious, as well as the complexity of his choice mechanisms can be blithely ignored if one wants to live in the baroque age of Ignatius. Most of us do not wish this. On the other hand, we would have acquired our modern knowledge at too high a price if it had us reduce everything that goes on in our psyches to merely psychological phenomena. A fruitful study could be done on the close connection there is between the penchant of Satan to remain inevident and the difficulty most of us have in identifying our various feelings. The unwillingness or inability to face the latter leaves the former unexposed. As a result, the slavery too many men live under is not even evident to themselves.

A third reason for the failure of the *Spiritual Exercises* of Ignatius to be of assistance to more Christians is implicit in the word "discernment." It implies that God has an already determined will for me in all its particulars and that it is merely my own inability to perceive it that has me fail to conform to it. From human experience we know that any relationship that has one of the partners inflicting an unending series of predetermined decisions on the other is doomed either to dissolution or to the subjugation of one of them. It is hard to know why we insist on conceiving God's relationship with us in such unloving terms, but we do. Although revelation reveals a Father, our own misunderstandings often make Him sound like a Divine Determinist. The phrase that encapsules this distortion is "God's will for me."

God has a very definite and particular will for His creatures: that they be and become what He has made and is making and that they avoid what mars His handiwork. Indeed, He wills to bring to completion the salvation wrought in and through His Son, Jesus. But as a person is drawn into the ambit of His love—"I have not called you servants but friends"—we move away from a relationship that is concerned with and focused on the "oughts" and "ought nots" that God's will meant in that religious and psychological phase of development. To the extent that an actual relationship of love develops between a man and God, to that extent God's will and mine conspire. This is what the Spirit, received in men, makes possible. God's will comes to me from the sense of congruence that develops in the relationship of love. It does not mean that He ceases to have definite choices that He wills for me; love does not make us equals. But it usually means that my choice, when developed in love, is very much my own and is very much His at the same time. "We" choose. When He foresees difficulties with the choice, He shows His nonconfirmation by some kind of dissonance at the affective level of my being. His overriding concern is not primarily with the particulars of my choosing but that these particulars be made within the faith context that His love and His Spirit are creating in me.

Barring the case of the second client, the "out-of-the-blue" call to this or that, a person's choices are made responsibly and freely if done in the context already described. This means that the following conditions obtain: The object of my choice is morally good; it is taken not on the basis of my own egotism and the willfulness that would be its sign; my own heart has been brought, by God's grace, to the point of equilibrium or indifference about the object of my choice and, therefore, it is not chosen for its own sake in isolation from Him; and He confirms the choice by some indication of His pleasure. My choices are wrong, on the other hand, if they are unfree and made outside of this context. They are unfree if their content is sinful. They can also be unfree if they are taken in an aseptic atmosphere that has failed to detect or come to grips with or disregards the feelings of the person. This would be a formal choice for unreality in the name of God. Any choice taken in such an atmosphere is a wrong choice, because it is either no choice at all or an option to go against what He has made.

A choice is not His will if taken irresponsibly, that is to say, if it is not taken as a means conducive to pursuing the end for which the person was made and to which he is being called. The retreat increases the retreatant's sensitivity to the dynamics that influence his choices. It enhances the possibility that he can sort out these influences in this given instance and thus arrive at a decision that will glorify God (since disordered affections will not have determined it), while at the same time his affectivity will have registered the most important data in the entire process of the decision making.

The experience of the conflicting spirits should prove most helpful long after the retreat has been completed. Just as an unawareness of these may, in the past, have led him to deny that such influences are affecting him, so the experience will help him to get in touch with the feeling level of his person. Rather than lapse back into insensitivity about the moods that come over him, or a disregarding of them, Ignatius would enjoin the retreatant to be most assiduous in examining himself regularly, about his fidelity in being open to God's inbreaking love and the affective course of his thoughts and feelings. A constant scrutiny of the desolation that leads to a discouragement about walking with the Lord and of the consolation that lightens our step in our walking with Him will be of immense help in understanding how he is being led and by what he is being influenced. It is this personal experience, aided by God's grace, that will begin to make one adept in the discernment of spirits, first in himself and then in others.

f. The Absence of Signs

The fourth man to come to Ignatius to seek help in discovering the way for him to follow his Lord and Savior has been brought to the point where he wishes to make a major decision about the disposition of his life. He has the necessary attitude toward created reality so that he will not allow himself to make a choice merely on the basis of his attraction, nor will repugnances be the final determinants about the object of choice being weighed. Ignatius will first inquire whether his heart is tranquil or not. If it is not, he would discourage his pursuing the decision at the present time. When he is experiencing turmoil of soul, no decision is to be taken, Ignatius informs him. He is merely to persevere in the good resolves he had before he entered into such a period, until the agitation subsides.

Nor, by the same token, is he experiencing any notable consolation, a situation both he and his director would prefer, but neither of them are able to induce such feelings nor can they demand that God bestow His felt presence.

What is one to do, given the fact that there are no detectable data coming from the level of the person's affectivity? What Ignatius proposes to him is a discursive, methodical approach to the choice being contemplated. While observation of the affective stages the person was undergoing was the key to determining the call of the previous client, the key instrument for this client will be his own reasoning: not that he is to deduce the choice from general principles, but that his faith-enlightened reason is to play the major part in seeing what is the better course for him to follow, the choice that is more for God's greater honor and glory. In the place of the horizon of inbreaking love felt by the previous client, this man's horizon must be brought up close by much prayer, considering the end for which he was created, the salvation of his soul through the praise, reverence, and service of God. His choice is to be made no less in the context of the love of God than the previous man's, but since this is not felt, the horizon must be made present through reflection and memory.

Several scenes are also suggested by Ignatius so that the purpose for which his client was created can be more concretely, even visually, operating as the horizon in which his choosing will take place. He is to view the contemplated choice from the perspective of his imagined deathbed and try to sense what the choice would look like from that point in time. Or he might find it profitable to see himself before the Judge upon his entrance into eternity and imagine the presently contemplated choice in the light of that moment. He might find it profitable, Ignatius informs him, to weigh the matter with pencil in hand, listing the advantages on the one hand and disadvantages on the other of the proposed choice in the light of the end for which he was created. As in the previous client's case, he will gradually come to sense the harmony or incongruence of his choice over against the background of God's drawing him to Himself.

The person has been brought to maximal openness by God's grace about what seems to him the most important choice in his life, and as far as he can see, God does not reveal His "will" to him nor indicate to him the vocation He would have him follow. Furthermore, the push and pull of conflicting spirits are not revelatory of the choice he should make. God's will is what his own good Christian sense concludes to. His will is *that* he choose and *how* he chooses; what he chooses is, for some and at times, a matter of indifference to God, it seems. God's will is that he accepts his having been loved and chosen and that all his choosings be made in the light of this love, whether this is felt, as in the previous case, or construed through faith-enlightened reason, as in this one. God's will is that he choose those means which, as far as one can perceive in faith, will be the most effective in bringing him to the full presence of love to which He is beckoning him.

Having chosen what seems to be the right thing for him to do with his life, he will ask God to show His acceptance of the decision by confirming it. Ignatius tells him "to turn with great diligence to prayer in the presence of God, our Lord, and offer Him the choice that the Divine Majesty may deign to accept and confirm it if it is for His greater service and praise." In view of the absence of a word heard from without about the best choice for him, he has determined as far as he can see with his "natural powers" what that should be. Ignatius is sure that since the decision was weighed in an explicit faith-context, God will in some way indicate His pleasure or displeasure with it. The retreatant is told that he can expect that there will be some indication of God's response to his choice, since he has done his best to make his choice in the context of his relationship with God.

If the contemplated choice runs counter to what is best for the choosing person and he cannot see this at the moment, then it will be made clear to him by a nonconfirmation of the choice. By withholding a sense of fittingness or rightness about it, God will indicate a given choice to be a poor one and, consequently, wrong for him. By increasing the sense of rightness or fittingness initially felt, or by any other form of consolation He may choose, such as peacefulness or a sense of His presence, God shows His confirmation of a good choice, one that is an apropos means for the retreatant to take to serve and glorify Him.

By so acting, He seems to be dealing with us as a good Father would; as sons made in His image and likeness, He invites us to use our freedom and assume responsibility for our choices, while protecting us from the unseen dangers that wrong choices taken in openness to Him and trust in Him could involve.

So much for the general criteria and particular rules for detecting the presence or absence of the activity of the Holy Spirit. If used with a healthy respect for the mystery of God's dealings with man, they will be of some help. This attitude of respect for mystery is called for because of the Person of the Spirit who, like the wind, can do unpredictable things, whenever and howsoever It pleases. Advice such as these pages on discernment contain can sound like formulas for a successful rain dance if taken too literally or applied too rigidly.

In the final analysis, it is the Spirit Itself Who teaches men the art of discernment by teaching them to love the One into whose Presence they have been led. Particular choices, then, are taken in terms of their primordial choice: to accept God's love of them. Given a relationship with God that is Spirit-knit, "a man can judge the value of everything, and his own value is not to be judged

by other men" (I Cor. 2:15). There is nothing of God's
will, or that God wills men to know, that will be unknown
to men "for the Spirit reaches the depths of everything,
even the depths of God" (I Cor. 2:10).